33 WAYS NOT TO SCREW UP CREATIVE ENTREPRENEURSHIP

SAUDIA DAVIS

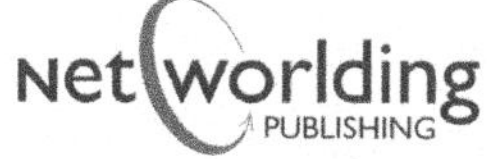

*"Instead of causing trouble,
go cause transformational opportunities today!"*

MELISSA G WILSON, PRESIDENT, NETWORLDING & NETWORLDING PUBLISHING

Networlding Publishing, Inc. Chicago, IL

www.networlding.com

33 Ways Not to Screw Up Creative Entrepreneurship—1st ed.

Print - 978-1-955750-19-6

eBook - 978-1-955750-20-2

CONTENTS

INTRODUCTION

It was a lovely fall afternoon in Chicago when I met Bob Gabriel. There were crisp ocean-blue skies—not too hot by day, and just a slight chill at night. Bob was an education executive who, over time, graciously supported my non-profit, Smarty Pants Are Leaders. He also was superb at inviting key influencers to meet one another to explore potential, mutually beneficial opportunities. Such was the case when he asked me to be one of several guests at a Chicago Blackhawks game. It was at this event that I had the good fortune of meeting Melissa Wilson.

When Melissa and I met, I recognized her from Bob's workshop I attended a year prior. She was on a three-person panel, and the topic was *Connectors, How They Work.* Melissa was the dynamic publisher who sat between my mentor, Fred Siegman, and Billy Dexter, another world-class networker, like Fred. I had the opportunity to speak with her briefly after the talk, and she autographed the book she wrote called *Networking is Dead.* Wow, how cool it was to hang out with her at the Blackhawks game. As a result of that splendid meeting we became fast friends, meeting regularly to network over coffee.

During one of these meetings Melissa recommended, as a best-selling author who had now turned into a publisher, that I write a book. But, at that time, I was not at all confident with the idea. But I recalled a conversation with a sage writer who had once given me some strong advice. This was when I had the honor of having dinner with Dr. Toni Morrison at one of my friend's South Side home. Dr. Morrison was an editor before she became known for her writing. Our mutual friend Dr. Rudy Lumbard, another wonderful influencer similar to Fred and Bob, invited me to join this fabulous dinner where he was cooking his Louisiana Gumbo, which was straight out of his cookbook *Creole Feast* which is the book that Dr. Toni Morrison edited.

She happened to be in town to receive an award, and his gumbo was her favorite. At dinner, Dr. Morrison and I talked about her work and what motivated her to write one of her best-selling books, *Sula*. She shared with me that she had received thirteen *No*(*s*) from publishers before she got a *Yes*. She further shared that it was not until she turned 40 that she wrote *Sula*. After she offered the insight about her age, she asked me, how old are you? I told her, and she responded, "Well, Honey, you haven't lived long enough to have anything to say yet!" We both laughed. Something about Dr. Morrison's statement rang out like wake-up alarm when Melissa suggested I write a book. But at that moment, I still wasn't ready yet.

But then two years later, The Kehrein Center for the Arts, a 1000-seat theatre auditorium I developed on Chicago's West Side after it sat dank and gutted for forty-five years, opened its doors to a mayoral race and then again in the fall for "Invest South West." On this day, the city of Chicago also launched a significant initiative to support disinvested communities. I experienced the vision I had put forth with a dedicated team come to life. I finally had something to say. I called Melissa. I was ready! And yet, it still took me another year.

But here we are . . . now.

This book is like a deliciously seasoned *creole feast* gumbo with all of the soulful stories, people, and places peppered in for your delight. It's also a treasure trove of insights I've collected because of the many superb influencer colleagues who so graciously shared their best insights. I hope you find that reading this book feels like you're sitting with me having a cozy fireside chat. Finally, I'll also share my expertise along with further wisdom from a variety of tech innovators, inventors, and other creative entrepreneurial colleagues.

I hope these pages will provide the critical guidance to light your path. Being a *creative* can often feel lonely as you may find you tend to hang out inside your head a lot. Creatives definitely like and benefit from their alone time as it often takes that special time to put their thoughts into action. Additionally, no one can hold the vision for your company like you can. But after years of helping creatives realize their potential, I have taken the time to develop a robust set of practices, processes, and resources for you. In this book, I'll share as many as I can. Don't worry. You are not alone. I've got your back.

HOW TO USE THIS BOOK

Each chapter has been strategically numbered in the order of what you may encounter in your progress towards your creative business development. Sometimes I open up a book and read the page that I land on. I also encourage you to try this. You may find a particular chapter has a technique you need at the moment you open the book. So have fun with it, and don't take me or yourself too seriously.

#1 RELATIONSHIPS (ARE) RESOURCES

Most people think that building strategic relationships is a highly valuable skill. However, some may regard this skill as taking advantage of others. But if you consider those powerful relationships that offer both parties new and exciting opportunities for each other, then you are at a higher level of relationship building. I have seen many creative entrepreneurs build extremely successful businesses based on making solid, warm connections and then discerning key opportunities for one another as a result.

This is all about building "social capital." It's a real thing. Here, individuals can effectively monetize their relationships. Then it is these relationships that become resources to others. Early on in my creative entrepreneurship development, one of my trusted advisors encouraged me to monetize my relationships.

Fred Siegman, whom I referenced in the introduction, is called the Serial Connector. (™) He has built a successful business for many years connecting individuals and companies. First, he identified that my brain works like a matrix. You tell me a name, and my mind synthesizes and spits out a connection point. Fred realized that I had unique high-profile relationships with known politicians, reputable celebrities, social influencers, business leaders in sports, and the public and private sector.

I'll never forget what Fred said: "You have the kind of relationships that people would pay you to make introductions to them." I created an LLC called Connectivity Point as a result of Fred's statement to me.

Fred taught me how to understand the value of my relationships and the possibility of monetizing them. In reflection, I discovered that I had value because I began to consider how many connections I had made between individuals and businesses in the past. I watched them grow with successful financial outcomes. However, after initial conversations with my new business, Connectivity Point, regarding my "contract," I didn't like the implications of what that would potentially do to my relationships.

I want to be trusted. Trust is important to me, and I value a friend's trust over the cost of connecting someone else to them. I opted out. I pulled back and decided not to monetize my relationships. I dissolved Connectivity Point, LLC. and continued to nurture my valuable relationships.

I asked my dedicated mentor, Fred Siegman, to contribute his expertise to this chapter, and he shared the following:

"Relationships open the doors to business and career opportunities and lead to friendships. So how do you maximize this key resource?

You will always have relationships that start and grow randomly. Adding a strategic approach to your relationship development will have a great impact on your results.

Step 1: Set a goal. Why do you want to build relationships? If you think carefully about the question, you might come up with 20 or 30 possible reasons. Three of the most common are lead generation, career advancement, or perhaps you've just relocated and want to make new friends. By the way, you can have more than one goal simultaneously with different additional steps.

Step 2: Identify targets. Targets could be specific individuals or groups that you want to connect to meet your goal. For example, you may want to meet people in a particular industry or people who share the same interest as you, like modern art or a specific sports team.

Step 3: Create strategies and actions to connect with your targets. If I want to meet an individual, my usual first step is identifying people I know who know my target. Another option is to identify a place where I will have an opportunity to meet my target, like an organization luncheon that my target is involved in.

Regarding connecting to people in a specific organization, I love trade associations and trade-related professional organizations. Pick your industry. Almost all have an association and multiple organizations. I've never found an industry without its own association.

On the personal side, you can find places that will attract people who share your interest. For example, multiple museums offer programs in addition to their exhibits. There are fan clubs and other gathering spots for every sports team. You can take classes on the subject of your interest, perhaps photography.

Step 4: What will you say when you meet a target or someone randomly? This last step done poorly will negate all the previous ones. You typically have about 5-10 seconds to engage someone when you meet them. Like all elevator pitches, there are three parts: attention getter, content, and memory maker.

When a potential connection is made, you have the luxury to plan what you will say. There isn't room here to explain this in detail. However, I will offer one bit of advice. Make your attention-getter and content as much as possible about the person you're connecting with, and you will be much more likely to start a relationship successfully.

Regarding randomly meeting people, the most common exchange is, "How do you do? What do you do?" Think of ways to introduce yourself other than stating, "I am a consultant, engineer, accountant..." and so on. One client I worked with started introducing himself as, "I build bridges between the United States and Asia." When someone asks what that means, he tells them he is an international trade attorney, and the conversation was off and running, and the relationship potentially beginning.

You can let all your relationships start randomly, or you can begin using strategic relationship development to add targeted connections to your relationship network."

When people ask me what I do, my short answer is: "I'm a Producer/Developer of content and physical spaces." But a more defined answer is: I create spaces and places for creatives to play, either on-screen or on a stage.

To Fred's point, relationship building can be calculated for a strategic result. Note that I'm not talking about a *manipulative* result. Again, it's about mutually beneficial relationships. This is a practice that requires some prep work. Develop your elevator pitch. As he states, "You have only 5-10 seconds to engage someone when you meet them. I suggest you make it a lasting first impression. Make it sticky so that they remember you. Something that distinguishes you from all of the people they've met, *period!*"

Let's delve into your friendships which could become resource partners. Where do you draw the line? There's a distinction. Call it a sweet nuance between maintaining your friendship within those relationships and not compromising your friendship. You run the risk of damaging your relationships by making people feel like you're going to apply a value to their friendship with you by monetizing it.

That's the subtle nuance. It breaks the unspoken authentic trust between you. That's not why we connect with people as friends. Now, if it is strictly business, be sure to make it clear. Start your business connections with an agreement first. That way, if an authentic friendship develops, it will have safeguards to develop naturally with healthy boundaries.

Establishing your social capital is a fine dance of transparency and confidentiality. There have been times where I've protected certain relationships with highly visible individuals, and in most cases, with what would be considered highly valuable resources. You can also jeopardize your reputation and become known for only having *transactional* relationships. There is no question. As Melissa shares in her process called *Networlding*, building transactional relationships will more likely than not result in *limited opportunities* for both partners.

Like plants take in carbon dioxide and, in return, they give us oxygen, great networking opportunities come from true partnerships where both parties want to give more than request. This will amplify and leverage the economic vitality of your relationship. It's a reciprocal relationship that also is an *ongoing exchange.*

When I met Melissa, she was on a panel discussing the subject she had authored five books on—networking. She helped me better understand that *you* don't connect people unless you see the connections as *significant* for both parties.

Along with her on the panel was her co-author Billy Dexter. They wrote one of the top-selling networking books. Billy is an executive and a top networker himself, and Fred was also on the panel. The three of these top Chicago networkers have referred one another to many others throughout the years, making them what Melissa terms *Networlders.*

During the panel discussion, Billy made the observation, "I believe when networking you have a responsibility to make *quality, mutually beneficial connections.*" He then said to Fred, "You don't call or email me often asking me for a connection, so when you do reach out, I know that it is significant, and I respond."

Fred replied, "And I am the same with you. When you do call, I know it must be significant."

NOTE: Don't make your relationships transactional as then they will only be temporary instead of expansive, and, more succinctly, "opportunity-expansive," per Melissa.

There is a fine line of understanding when not to have this transactional expectation within your relationships. It's almost like you have to know when to turn it on when you're in business mode and when to turn it off when you're at home. I've experienced unconsciously having transactional relationships which do not expand and do not grow, or the person feels that they're needed in an unhealthy way. People, your friend or your partner, will not feel loved, but rather you may come across as "conditional."

They may begin to feel that you need them for a reason instead of being in a relationship to just be in a relationship with them. So it's a nuanced space where you may choose to connect the dots. If you choose to use your relationships as resources, here's my caution: consider your personal, dynamic relationships first, and then, just like you turn off your computer at the end of the day, you turn off that connection expectation in your personal relationships.

Can you imagine? If you get into relationship-building for

resources, it can potentially leak into your personal versus professional relationships. Speaking from experience, it's a horrible feeling when you realize your loved ones feel that there's an expectation lingering on the other side. There's something to be said about unconditional love, right?

We can get so caught up in our business, especially when we are stressed. The lines can blur easily. I learned that I was not turning off my business side once at home in private time. So my cautionary tale to you is this: Be sure to check in with yourself. You'll find this in chapter 7, " Being on Purpose in Your Life."

You must learn how to listen to yourself before you listen to others. This is not about being selfish. It's about trusting your gut. Not everyone will tell you that you are the asshole in the room. It's up to you to know how you impact other people, just like you are conscious of how others impact you.

People often ask how I know so many people or how I got connected to such a person. I will tell them that it's more work than you realize. In chapter 10, "Introvert-Extrovert," I explain how if it's not natural to you, it is okay because relationship building, what some call networking, is a learned skill.

I recently had a friendship where we went into business. When we decided to go into business, we created a contract right away to create healthy boundaries. I hired this individual to consult me on the industry in which she was more advanced than I. I know what my strengths and weaknesses are, and if I have a weakness, I will find a friend, relationship, or resource with expertise.

But the process of working together created some insecurities in both of us. This person felt that there might be conflicts with some of the people with whom we were working that could affect their business. As a result, our trust in one another became compromised.

Also, other nuances of misunderstandings led us to have less trust in each other. So we decided to stop working together to maintain our friendship. So when resources that are your relationships are dynamic, they are not to be taken for granted. Your relationships matter, *and* your resources matter.

Now some resources do not necessarily include a relationship connected to the resource. But what I find most exciting is when a resource becomes a relationship. Sometimes you do business with a particular company, and the clients you meet there are only resources at first. But by discerning your common values, interests, and goals, you evolve your relationship into a significant partnership.

#2 ORGANIZATION - SKATTERIZATION

On a scale of 1-10, how organized are you? Do you make your bed when you get up in the morning? Do you clean up the kitchen after your breakfast, even if it's just coffee? Or do you leave your coffee cup or dishes in the sink before you start your day? Do those dishes that you left from the morning flow into the afternoon or into the evening and then multiply into the next day?

Is your desk orderly or in complete chaos? I'm asking these key questions because they are potential indicators of your ability to organize. Routines and order around you can suggest your ability to be organized in your business. Maria Condo is a success for so *many* reasons! Organization or for what I call "Skatterization?"

Have you ever heard the saying: what's going on inside is a reflection of your outside? Or one could also say what is going on on the outside is a reflection of what's going on the inside. Believe it or not, your ability to organize can influence how you communicate with others. It can determine the sustainability of your creative endeavor.

If the area around you is not orderly, there's a strong possibility that your thoughts and vision for the day could potentially be as disorderly. Therefore you may not communicate clearly with your team, your partner, or your lovemate. You may say, "Oh, although my physical space may be out of order, I seem to be communicating fine with my team, my partner, or my love mate." But are you really?

Skatterization defines this attribute of my *friends* out there who believe they are organized but are totally scatterbrained. Because of that, there are breaks in communication. They find themselves not running on time, they miss important details in meetings because they are all over the place, and eventually, all of these things fall through the cracks. And with time, those fissures or cracks manifest into huge misunderstandings. Worst of all, they can create the end of a contract or the dissolution of your business.

If you are a creative person like me, your mind moves fast. Before one genius thought comes to mind, another equally brilliant thought is forcing its way through. For this reason, I make it a priority to create boundaries, routines, and rituals. I create order in my mind by writing down those ideas or make a voice recording of them on my iPhone.

I keep my home or office tidy. What this means is that I make my bed every morning, freshen up the main living room, and while making breakfast, I clean at the same time. After my coffee, I put the cup in the dishwasher.

I do my best to keep the area around my computer clear. If I get super busy, I can be "a stacker." Here, mini-intentional stacks of important documents may rise on my desk, but I set a time to get to them, then I file and clear them as quickly as possible.

I believe this is important because, in order for you to see clearly, you must have a clear space. I understand that the counter-argument is that as a creative entrepreneur, you thrive in chaos. Some people do. Okay, so you like it messy! It's your vibe! But here's the thing: it may be your vibe, but ultimately, it will not serve you.

Skatterizers thrive in Skatterization. They believe that disorder somehow assists in their creative process. Trust me. It might work for a while because it is what they/you know to have been your process when they/you reached a "level" of success.

I'll give you an example of a type of creative that uses emotion to inspire their process. Now, I am not judging or stating a truth for everyone who uses the process I will use in examples. Songwriter-singers and some actors are good examples. There are some songwriter-singers who are only able to write when there is a truth to the sad song that they produce. Unfortunately, there are lag times between their projects because the inspiration that drives their process is not there!

Some actors use "Method Acting."[1] This technique requires that actors drop into a deeply sad lived traumatic experience in order to deliver a human experience in an imaginary circumstance to connect with the character and deliver the most believable performance.

In the early 20th century, a Russian actor/director, Konstantin Stanislavski, invented the technique. Although he did not call it "the Method," his creation provided a model for actors designed to help them call upon personal memories and experiences in the development of their characters. This was extremely innovative in its day, contrasting greatly with the previous theatrical, traditional and classical acting methods that came before.

Gurus of the 1930s acting studios, including Elia Kazan and Lee Strasberg, developed it further and introduced The Method to American actors. It's about completely immersing oneself in the role of the character and is emotion-based as opposed to classical acting, which is primarily action-based. Famous actors who follow The Method in their work include Dustin Hoffman, Robert DeNiro, Marlon Brando, Charlize Theron, Angelina Jolie, Al Pacino, Kate Winslet, Hillary Swank, and Christian Bale, just to name a few.

As a trained actor myself, we call it "substitution." Now, both of these are highly effective processes that have proven successful. Grammys and Oscars are awarded based on the level of distress/angst that was engaged in order to produce this kind of work. Some individuals who work this way have difficulties separating from the darkness of the character. For example, some say Heath Ledger had a difficult time detaching when he played The Joker in *The Dark Knight*.

I feel I must also mention Robert Downing, Jr., who immerses himself in his characters quite often, such as his performances in *Chaplin, Sherlock Holmes,* and *Iron Man*. He went through years of well-known struggles with addiction in his personal life, but because he was so talented even when impaired, directors still wanted to work with him.

He's been clean and sober for several years now, but here are a couple of his quotes about addiction: "Smoking dope and smoking coke, you are rendered defenseless. The only way out of that hopeless state is intervention." With his great sense of humor, he has also said, "I don't drink these days. I am allergic to alcohol and narcotics. I break out in handcuffs."[2]

Many people use drugs and/or alcohol to cope with the depression that they can't shake. We hear about this in our creative community all of the time. In fact, both film and music industries have historically, off the record, supported the bad habits of their creatives in order to elicit the desired outcome. Remember, it's about business, and there is always a bottom line.

Just because there is an appearance of success doesn't mean

that they have a winning formula for success. I want you to win. And clearly stated, I want you to have fun and not feel like "It's business."—even though it is the cost of doing business.

So if you answered yes to the Skatterization questions, try something different. Try creating your own system of organization that makes sense for you. But make it a routine. It's said that if you do anything for 21 days straight, it creates a new behavior. Here's why, when you create space by clearing out, considering the idea that "less is more," your intuition will kick in, and the clarity that you have created in the physical space will allow for clarity in your mental space.

What's your Magic Hour? I define the Magic Hour as the time or place at which your most creative inspiration starts flowing. This is a thing. My Magic Hour is at 4 am. It's when lyrics flow effortlessly, a scene or an entire script for a movie comes through; it's when the seeds for innovation are planted.

Some people I know find this effortless flow in the water while taking a shower or swimming. Even at this moment, you have to create boundaries for yourself. For me, if I wake up at 4 am with inspiration, I will work until 6 am, then take a nap and wake back up at 8 am. I know this may sound weird, but you can also ask yourself to be reminded of *this inspiration* in the morning so that you can sleep more soundly. Generally, I've learned to get up and "deliver the goods." Then I find a time to sleep later. The key is making sure that you have enough rest to stay energized and fresh in your creativity.

In terms of getting organized, most smartphones have calendars with reminders. Use it. If you are a paper person, write your appointments down. Keep a thought keeper or journal. Keep the area around your bed clear. If you can, keep underneath your bed clean and clear. For folks with storage issues, I get it. But do your utmost to make the best of the limited space you have.

Have you heard of the Native American ritual, "Smudging," clearing negative energy by burning dry herbs like Sage or lavender? Smudge sticks are woven-tied herbs that can be purchased at Whole Foods. I recommend you try it, and if you like it, consider "*smudging*" every two weeks. Sage smudging unblocks stuck energy. As far as making space for your ideas to clearly come through, this also works for a mate. I'll never forget my best friend Celine was frustrated with her one large closet in her New York Tudor City apartment. To motivate her, I suggested that she consider that "Guy" who had not yet shown up in her life; that she makes room for his things. And guess what? She met her now-husband shortly after she cleared out her frustrations, i.e., her closet.

Another example is a client in New York whose home I staged for sale. This was after my HGTV show *Splurge and Save*. I got a call from a real estate broker friend of mine, Eric. He called me in a bit of a panic. He said, "Saudia, I need your help immediately." Well, it was perfect timing because anytime is a good time for unexpected cash/income.

He shared that one of his clients (named Michelle) had a thing for purple and that everything—I mean *everything*—in her home was purple. I told him my rate and swung by to take a look. Not only was he not kidding, but I've also never seen anything like it. The carpet was Barney Purple, the sofa too, and the walls were every version of Purple, Lilac, and Lavender, except her child's room, which was Pepto Bismol pink.

There was little light in the space, and so with the oversized Barney huggable furniture, there was no way a buyer could see the beauty of the unit. I felt compelled to help. But I also liked Michelle, the owner. She was darling. She allowed me and my contractor to design and renovate the unit completely.

While Eric was reeling with despair and distrust that he would be able to sell the unit, I met with Michelle. I gave her an assignment. I said, "Come up with a date that you want to sell the unit. Do not tell anyone. You can tell me if you like, and I will hold the space for you to send positive confirming energy for your desired outcome."

She told me the date. And based on the short but fairly reasonable deadline (I knew my contractor, and I could get it done), she did not have enough time to read the books I would suggest. So although I gave her a couple of book suggestions, for the sake of time, I printed out excerpts of The Writings of Florence Scovel Shinn who wrote, *The Game of Life and How to Play It* and *Your Word is Your Wand,* along with Deepak Chopra's, *7 Spiritual Laws of Success,* and an oldie but goodie, *Key to Yourself* by Venice Bloodworth.

Not only did she sell on the date that she initially chose, but there was also a bidding war. The building was so impressed by the features that we added that they hosted a building tenant walkthrough. The singer Freddie Jackson fell in love with my design and insisted that we renovate his unit. Due to travel and his busy schedule, we did not design his unit. But he was a doll and invited me to a couple of performances.

Michelle was so thrilled and beside herself that she asked me to help her with her next project. She wanted me to design a bed for her. I did. She also shared that she wanted a man/partner! I had already equipped her with the tools she needed to magically manifest. I worked with Conor Mehan, a dear friend of my Godbrother who made custom wood furniture. I designed a lovely platform bed that quietly resembled a high heel shoe. She loved it. To this day, I still have the original rendering of the bed. Michelle later informed me that not only did she meet a man, she got married.

"When someone tells me I'm organized, I look at them like they have two disorganized heads. I'm not, partly because my brain's all over the place, but I do consistently fight to bring order to desktop chaos. If it's in my head and I like it, I write it down--on post-it notes, yellow legal pads, or the note app on my iPhone. I may not always remember *where* I write it down, but it's findable (if you don't write it down, no matter how good it is, you'll forget it, especially if you have creative ADD). Once a week or so, I do a street sweep of my desktop. I look at each piece of paper to see if there's anything worth recording somewhere more permanent. It's a pain in the file cabinet, but there's nothing worse than knowing you had a good idea and now it's gone forever."

CLIO AWARD WINNING CREATIVE DIRECTOR/ WRITER: ROBERT "BOB" MERLOTTI

1 Mayo, Alyssa. "How the Best Method Actors Prepare for Their Roles." Studiobinder.com. June 14, 2020. https://www.studiobinder.com/blog/what-is-method-acting

2 AZQuotes website. "Robert Downey, Jr. Quotes About Addiction." AZQuotes.com. Accessed August 30, 2021.

https://www.azquotes.com/author/4113-Robert_Downey_Jr/tag/addiction

#3 HARD STOP: POWER DOWN

Even before the pandemic, a dear friend with a focus on women's health informed me that there was a significant increase in highly successful women presenting to the E.R. with unexplainable symptoms. During a talk I moderated on entrepreneurship, I asked one question of three women and one man among our panelists. But allow me to preface it with what I shared with the audience.

"I was recently alerted by the Apple Store that my computer must be put to sleep, just like we must sleep, or like us, it will crash. Here's the question: How do you make a hard stop? What are your routines around rest, recovery, and recharging? How do you power down?"

To my surprise and the audience's gasp of shock, the first answer was not what I expected to hear. Mary, we will call her, shared something extremely personal. She told us that unfortunately, because she did not know how to stop, she simply never did. She explained that she had been checked into the hospital, at which point they thought maybe she was having a panic attack at the very least, and at the most, maybe she had experienced a stroke because she could not talk or form her words.

And if anyone meets Mary, a power attorney, you'll soon discover that she's a talker! Mary, fortunately, made a major shift in her career.

Next up, Mikayla Johnson said, "Wow, Mary, that's really brave of you to share something so personal and intimate. Well, since we are being honest here, I too did not know how to stop, and a year ago, I nearly collapsed after not having slept for over 48 hours. I had to travel from Chicago to London and back to Chicago to pick up my bags for my trip to Los Angeles, where I received an ADCOLOR award.

By the time I made it to my hotel room, I could not stop crying. I called my physician sister and asked her what was wrong with me. I told her, 'When I started to write my acceptance speech, I couldn't write! I just started crying and shaking.' My sister said, 'Mikayla, you need to *stop*. You stay up every day until 4 am posting on Instagram, only to get up at 8 am. Although you have 500K followers, it's not worth risking your mental health.'" Mikayla barely made it through her awards ceremony. Upon her return to Chicago, her family held an intervention.

So although this may be news to you, it was a well-kept secret among highly successful women who were experiencing severe fatigue. I sought to shine a light on this and hosted Power Up to Power Down, a breakfast retreat for high-functioning ladies. I had a moment to speak with Cecil Roberts, who shared that she was hearing more and more about this, and as soon as she had a moment to take a break, she would like to speak with me.

The same day at this same event, Senator Jan Schakowsky sat me down and told me a story that helps her "power down." Suffice it to say, you should count the good things that you accomplished in your day. Not ones that you did not complete that will keep you up worrying and beating yourself up. Instead, give thanks to yourself and celebrate your wins.

So, I ask you: How do you power down from your day? Do you know how to make a hard stop? You have heard of setting the expectation in a meeting to a hard stop, right? Well, you must set the expectation for yourself to create boundaries around your time and be sure to create a specific time that you end your day, hard stop from working. Be consistent, and that way, you set the expectation with your partners for the time your workday ends.

#4 HIGH TOUCH IN HIGH TECH

We have to have technology, but we don't have to live and die by it. I believe in the power of technology. Almost every modern convenience we have is powered by some form of technology. As a former member of 1871, the Number 1 tech incubator in the world, which is based in Chicago, I can tell you that it has been the breeding ground for some of the most groundbreaking tech companies, like Steven Galanis' Cameo.

I have a lot of respect for the founders of such companies who have these moments of genius and push their ideas forward. I use Cameo as an example because of the creative nature of the business. It's also a great example of high touch. It's a brilliant way to connect people with their most desired crush/star/celebrity for a quick message. But what it does for the recipient, albeit I would argue for the famous person as well, is it creates a wonderfully memorable, heartfelt experience.

Another way to consider high-touch in high-tech is finding a balance between our tech-enabled world and the simplicity of just being. Doing so can recalibrate your connection. Which sometimes means disconnecting from our hardware. For example, take a break from your smartphone, your computer, or your iPad. Playing around on Instagram or Facebook is not the kind of connection that I am referring to.

I mean actually staying connected to your friends in person, or if they are far away, picking up the phone and calling them. Using FaceTime or WhatsApp video calls to see a friend or family member is another great personal way to connect. The operative experience is for you to feel. FEEEELLL.

As creatives, so much of who we are and what we are inspires what we create. As human beings, most of us thrive by feeling, communicating, or touching other humans or our animals. Our creativity comes from staying connected to something or someone. It's not enough for you to post on Instagram or Facebook, dance on Tik Tok, or tweet. There are more meaningful ways to live an enriched life.

Yet, with all of these wonderful social media platforms, we have a false sense of being connected when really, we're very disconnected. In fact, I would argue that in some cases, this false sense of connection can leave you feeling displaced, experiencing "FOMO" (fear of missing out), depression, and loneliness. However you define your creativity, I would be willing to bet that you feel better and more nourished when you have the opportunity to sit with someone in person, have a meaningful conversation, or sit in the park and watch the butterflies dance. Give it a try once in a while, or take a walk by the shore and watch the waves lap one over another.

Entrepreneurship, at its core, entails finding solutions to problems. Quite often, we find that we are often alone in our endeavors. As creatives, some of us live in our imagination, which sparks the idea for a song, a book, or even a tech innovation. So it's really imperative to find ways to get out of your head and off of the high-tech hardware. To move from your head to your heart, start by scheduling time to do those things that will touch your heart as often as you can. I promise you will have more inspired thoughts the more that you give yourself the freedom to disconnect from tech.

Following are just a few of the ways for you to disconnect from high tech and connect to high touch:

- Read a really good book
- Practice Yoga
- Go hiking with a group
- Go horseback riding
- Join an intramural team sport
- Ride your bike
- Take a dance class
- Join a theatre company or take improv classes
- Write in your journal with an actual pen to real paper

#5 INTUITION INSPIRATION

The beauty of tapping into your intuition is not something that anyone can really describe. It is something that you discover with practice. You know that feeling when you have left your home, and you think, "Wait, did I turn off the stove in the kitchen, or did I unplug the iron?" Did you rush back only to find that you did leave the stove on, or the iron plugged in and on? The good news is that nowadays, irons have automatic shut-offs.

Or let's say you left a candle burning only to return and see that your gut feeling was correct. That little instinct can be described as the quiet, still, voice that resides in all of us.

The more time you take to disconnect, the more you will become more in tune with yourself. For those of you who know this, let this chapter serve as a refresher. As in the previous chapter, taking time to disconnect from "all the things" and reconnect with yourself will awaken your inner voice. I define that small, still voice as your *intuition.*

As you start to ideate around a business idea, be sure to remember that the initial vision was your intuitive inspiration. Inspiration is the driving force creating the magical manifestation. But it will be difficult to decipher the details if you are too busy to listen or if there is too much distraction. You could call distraction a different kind of noise.

Some entrepreneurs have the spark of an idea and then lose focus because they are not tuned in. It's like a radio frequency: the message coming through is deep, but due to the static, you may want to change the station. Have a bit of patience. You have to clear the static first before you change the channel. Sometimes we'll get multiple ideas! And it can be hard to determine which one to move forward on.

What you will find as you have more practice in discerning your intuition is that you will know which of the many ideas that come along is the most important idea to move on now and which ones you can save for later. I recommend keeping a journal for this reason. You can keep an Ideas Book where you write down different ideas that you want to explore over time and consider where you are in your living space and relationships.

If you do have multiple ideas streaming forward, ask yourself, "Which one should I focus on now?" And then just be still. Be patient. Wait for an answer. And when you get an answer, don't second-guess it.

I'll share with you the most heightened experience I've had regarding intuition inspiration. At the start of 2021, I meditated first for 20 minutes. I happen to practice Transcendental Meditation. Then I prayed. And when I say pray, I generally refer to myself as being more of a spiritual person than a religious person. So I asked the question to God, the universal, omnipresent, omnipotent, gracious Universal being, "What do I *really want*? What business can I do that will serve my highest good?"

The first and immediate response was an overwhelming flush of Grace and a GOOD feeling of gratitude, almost as if to say I heard, *"You're doing so good, you're really doing good work. If nothing else, you've done enough."* And then I had a spark of memory from 28 years ago.

I wanted to run a film studio. I was living in Los Angeles, working behind the camera in production and at times in front of the camera on commercials. I earned my Screen Actors Guild (SAG) card while working on a Marco Brambilla McDonald's commercial. The commercial was made for the movie *Armageddon* with Ben Affleck. My role involved sitting in the car with pre-academy award winner Naomi Watt. On that day, I had two jobs: I was both a production assistant (PA) and on-camera talent.

I thought I eventually wanted to run Paramount Pictures or Warner Brothers. At that time, I was young, I was ambitious, and there were a lot of distractions along the way. There was a lot of noise. I often took job opportunities to pay the bills, ever considering how far those job opportunities would take me from my intended goal. At one point, I was the assistant manager for the Mondrian Hotel, an Ian Schrager Hotel in Los Angeles.

I started a painting company called Pretty Painters, designing people's interior home walls based on holistic wellness. I always wanted a show on HGTV. I moved to New York and pitched Pretty Painters to my Agents at Abrams Artists. After auditioning for E! and MTV, and HGTV many times, I finally booked HGTV as a Host for *Splurge and Save.* I share these milestones to demonstrate that, in some cases, dreams manifest as distractions. Because although I stated that I wanted to run a film studio, nowhere along this journey could anyone have drawn a direct line to that vision.

Once I had that recollection, it occurred to me that two years ago, the director for the Illinois film office had shared with me that the state had two immediate needs. The state needed more film stage infrastructure and more workforce development to support the film business here in Chicago. I had just finished developing a Theatre on Chicago's West Side in the Austin community. Yet, I wasn't ready. I was distracted. I didn't consider that I could develop film stages at that time.

I took a contract working on entertainment with more workforce development in mind. At the same time, it was made clear to me that the Showtime show "Work In Progress" no longer had a home at the Hangar because it was rented, and therefore they needed somewhere else to film their series.

But they couldn't find anywhere to film and ended up utilizing space at Kennedy King College in the Englewood neighborhood on the South Side. Kennedy King is a community college. So I went back to my friend at the Illinois film office and asked, "So how is it going with film infrastructure?" I was informed that the problem had gotten worse because there was more demand for production companies to film in Chicago, but there was nowhere for film and TV shows to shoot.

I share this example with you because it is real and present. It demonstrates how circuitous the routes to success can be, especially when you are an entrepreneur. So my problem to solve became creating more film infrastructure here in Chicago. And guess what? Now I am ready. It occurred to me. I have the relationships, the access to capital, and the necessary resources as a producer. I understand the business of the business.

Here's my point. Because I asked the question and listened, the experience has been remarkably aligned. The pieces keep falling into place. More time is needed to determine the outcome. But what I will share is that I am focused. The vision that I had for myself 28 years ago on the other side of the country is coming together. I am in a position to provide opportunities to disinvested communities and returning citizens to realize wealth-generating jobs. I am able to support an industry that I love and have remained committed to. And I will not allow any distractions or noise to keep me from obtaining my goal.

Here's a story of another entrepreneur, Genevieve Thiers: Tech Innovator, Founder of Sitter City, to inspire you, in her own words:

> "When I was creating my company sittercity.com, I was laughed out of rooms constantly. And it was basically by men who had never hired a sitter in their lives. Their wives had done it. But I knew it would work. I had been a sitter for so long and exposed to so many desperate moms needing care and sitters like myself that needed work. It was just so obvious from my perspective we needed this.
>
> So I kept building. I literally fired on foot and hired friends, and talked to every parent I know. Soon female members of the press corps got a hold of it and they provided some amazing ballast. I never looked back and finally after raising $56 million in funding, serving over 10 million users and thousands of companies, and receiving 18 major awards, we sold to Bright Horizons last summer after 20 years of business."

#6 STICKY: IS YOUR VISION VALUABLE?

I'll never forget the first time I heard a tech company describe in a Brain Trust meeting how the company app needed to be "sticky." I've since heard this term used many times when referring to how apps and tech companies use algorithms to addict the user. Ultimately whether the brand is sticky is less relevant than if it provides a *value* in someone's life. Does your idea or company fill a gap in the business market? If yes, the *value relevance* will determine if people will buy your product or business.

Client retention is what it's all about. It's about what draws clients to your company. Are your services a necessity that creates a repetitive need? Being intentional about retaining business increases your odds of repeat business. A lot of people have good ideas, but it doesn't mean that your really good idea translates into a great business.

Do your diligence! Before you design a logo and invest in business cards or a website, have a brain trust or mini-brainstorming session with friends. Invite them over, serve food and drinks. By doing this you will get objective and honest feedback. You may also get early adopters or supporters for your new business. And ask them to consider:

- What problem does your idea solve and for who/what?
- Is there a need? If so, what is the percentage of market demand, local, national, or global?
- Is your business idea sustainable?

When developing a business you always have to consider: "What problem does it solve?" In order to define your place in the market you also need to determine who or what are you solving for. Again, a great idea is a great idea, but if there's no need for it and the market doesn't show a significant demand, then you're wasting a lot of your time and money. Because odds are, there's probably a company or companies that have already garnered their place in the market.

What sets your business apart? You may find that there are similar businesses in the market that are solving the same problem, but the demand may be high enough for your business to exist as well. If this is the case, then it's imperative that you determine what makes what you're offering different from what's already in the market, and then how much more specialized you can make it in order for it to be sustainable over time.

The more specialized and unique you can make the same idea that's out there in the market, the more you can create the sticky effect that you need. This is what will make people remember your brand and crave the difference your company offers. As Greg W. Reid, Health Tech Innovator Founder of Calibrated has this to say:

> "Vision is both the greatest attraction and fear for any businessperson to weigh in on. From personal experience, I

consider Vision as the ability to pre-determine the successful application of ideas and how those ideas will construct a future state of purposefulness. It requires courage to hold onto Vision, knowing that you alone are responsible for pulling everyone in your orbit to see through your secret peephole (Vision) that leads them to a promised land (Value) .

In fact, all created matter has value as it originates from our brain's impulse energy and is then blended with intense belief to make something new. I believe vision has intrinsic value to someone for some application, large or small. You just don't know how much value (purpose) it will offer.

As a content creator and product designer, I have seen my Visionary concepts move from one platform to another as its application was better suited. There will always be net-worth to ideas that are carefully placed in a setting or dimension that can accommodate it, and turn it into something useful (valuable) to service mankind. So yes, my vision and your vision is valuable."

#7 LEARN HOW TO LISTEN: BEING ON PURPOSE IN YOUR LIFE

The more business leaders I get to know, the more I find they have one thing in common. They have learned to follow their "gut." They have learned how to listen to what some may define as "instinct." Others may describe this experience as intuition. All of these experiences are somewhat the same.

I will always remember when I first discovered my gut. Some describe it as a feeling. In my case, it was a pain in my gut. I was living in New York, and my show on HGTV, "Splurge and Save," had recently been canceled. I went to the Gastroenterologist (GI) specialist. My Western medicine physician, Dr. Lee, happened to be of Chinese descent. He asked me if I knew what my gut was. He showed me a physical plastic model of the GI tract. He said, "Based on what you are describing, I think it's best that we schedule you for a colonoscopy to rule out Crohn's disease."

He went on to say, "We may also find that while you may not have a disease, you may be discovering your 'GUT.'" I asked what he meant. He continued explaining that there are organs that make up the gut, and then there is also our inner guidance center that makes up our "gut" feeling. Wow, it felt really cool to hear this from him.

I had just resigned from Hugo Boss shortly before my visit and therefore did not have health insurance at the time. He assured me that he would give me a "deep discount." I would like to thank him at this moment. I'll get back to the details of that later. Although I had a scheduled colonoscopy, it was a couple of weeks away. I decided during that time to return home to Chicago. I missed my family, and I wasn't feeling well.

My sister happens to be a Western Medical doctor as well. While I was visiting her home, I explained my pain. She did this stomach press test, and from the pain I felt, she believed it might be appendicitis. We went to Northwestern Hospital, and I was admitted immediately. To top it all off, it was the 4th of July weekend, and there I was, laid up in a hospital. My dearest sweet friend Nambi E. Kelly, playwright, extraordinaire, who at the time lived in New York and was always traveling, happened to be in Chicago came to visit me in the hospital. Our girlfriend chat was a great distraction from my uncertain situation.

The Gastric X-ray, MRI, or whatever the procedure was, involved me being pushed into a tube. The night before, I had to drink a nasty chalky, contrast solution. The results proved nothing more than inflamed intestines. Thankfully, no appendicitis—just an expensive 4th of July weekend laid up in a hospital bed hanging out with a dear friend.

Well, upon my return to New York, I had my scheduled colonoscopy. Guess what? After being a bit of a gassy girl, I was presented with photos of my colon in living color and informed by my doctor that I had the most beautiful colon. In fact, it was wonderfully healthy, just a bit inflamed. It was vibrant but, most important, polyp-free. No Crohn's disease!

Oh, and the doctor's "deep discount" was no charge! Free.

Wow, can you believe it? All true. So with a face full of tears, I thanked my doctor, and he said, "So here's the thing. You have discovered your 'gut!'" And to this day, when I am most in tune with myself or listening, and something is not quite right, or a person is not a good fit, I get a bit of a "pang"—a pinched feeling, a tightening clinch in my gut on the right side every time.

At that time, Deepak Chopra was a friend and advisor. I called him to tell him what I had just gone through. He then told me something that I live my life by to this day. In his authentic expert doctor voice, he said something like, "Saudia, you are holding onto a lot of anger from the loss of your show. Your body is in dis-ease." It's okay to set goals, but you must let go of any attachment to the outcome. You are trying to control things that cannot be controlled. When you allow yourself to go with the flow, the universe will open up and spontaneously manifest your heart's desire."

I asked him to put it in an email so that I would never forget it. He did.

I share this personal story not to brag about my experience but to provide credibility to what may seem like a very esoteric story. Albeit the truth, it is my experience. Everyone's experience is different. We all come to know ourselves in various ways. Some people overcome trauma, and through it, they find their internal compass. As a result, your compass is a self-guided tool that helps you determine without any outside influence if you are on the right path.

Do you know what your path is? Do you know your purpose? These are answers you need to know in order to discern if you are living your life's purpose. Being an entrepreneur doesn't necessarily mean that the business you create is your life's work. However, when you find the joy in doing what you love, some have said, "It's not working!"

What I will take a leap in asserting is that when you align

with being on purpose in your life, you will have a more unified and even effortless experience. Doors will open, and people say "yes" to you consistently. There are several books I would recommend if you are still searching. But for those of you who know why you are here and have created a business, or for those of you who do not subscribe to "being on your path" but who have created a business, I recommend the same thing: find time to be alone and listen.

It's not complicated. The trick is finding the time and the place to be completely quiet. You do not need to go away to an Ashram and volunteer your stay to do this, although I have many friends who speak highly of the experience. At first, silence may be uncomfortable. We are inundated with noise all the time, with TVs, radio, and advertisements that are intrusive, asking us to think about diagnosing everything. Add to that your friends, cell phone, and of course, social media FOMO.

If you are a Type A person like me (I don't like labels, but for the sake of understanding, I use this here), you may question why it's important to take time to be quiet. It took me years to learn how to meditate. But trust me when I tell you, the only way for you to hear yourself without getting freaked out is to learn what to listen for. Once you learn to *be quiet*, you will discover your best self.

Find a comfortable way to sit. Choose a comfy chair, sit on a mat or cushion. Sit up. I do not recommend lying down as you may fall asleep. We are all often fairly sleep-deprived in one way or another, but this is not the time to knock out. Rather I would suggest you close your eyes while sitting.

Begin by focusing on your breath. If you have taken any kind of yoga class, this will sound familiar. On each inhalation, listen to the air come into your body, and with each exhalation, listen to the air exit your body. Visualize your belly filling with the inhalation and caving empty with the exhalation. Your mind will gently wander, and that's okay. Allow it to be free to do so. Notice your thoughts but do not try to control them. Just relax.

Then listen. That's it. Listen. I suggest in the beginning keep a notepad nearby or your voice recorder on your cell phone. After you sit for 10 to 20 minutes, take note of the thoughts that enter.

What you will find over time is that this simple ritual or time that you set aside for yourself will pay you back with a massive ROI (return on investment). Once you begin to listen more and more, you will naturally begin to decipher your inner voice as opposed to outside influences. And as you listen more and more, you become more used to hearing yourself. Then I encourage you to trust your gut!

#8 MENTORS MATTER

Now that you know how to listen to yourself, it's time to get advice from others who are more advanced in your particular business and who can provide mentorship to you. Mentors matter. In fact, you can have a mentor at any age. The earlier, the better. I have learned as an adult, however, that many adults do not have mentors. What is the main reason why? They don't ask.

Don't worry! It's never too late, and there isn't an age requirement where you time out of this opportunity. Unlike in the first chapter on relationships as resources, mentors are a different kind of resource. They are a type of relationship based on an agreement. Just like every person is different, so is every mentoring relationship.

Do your research. Similar to seeking a job and then landing the interview, identifying a mentor is not terribly different. Show up on time, which is 15 minutes early. Consider the following things:

- Does the leader's field of practice align with you or your business?

- Are they reputable, credible?
- Do you know someone who can make a warm introduction?
- Ask for a 15-minute initial meeting.
- Tell them why you would like to speak with them.
- Be prepared to listen.
- Take notes even in your first meeting. It may be the only meeting you get.
- Ask informed questions. Prove to them that you did your research. They will appreciate you were astute enough to value their knowledge.
- Be specific and concise with your request or questions. This will honor their time.
- Be ready to follow their guidance if you believe it is applicable.
- Take what you can get. Bend your schedule to meet theirs.
- After your first meeting, you will have an idea if you want to schedule more time.
- If you do find value in meeting with this person, attempt to set a regular meeting time for 30 minutes. Allow him or her to tell you what works best for them and their schedule. They may schedule an hour with you.

You can always ask. You may not get a yes, but if you do, get ready to be responsible with this busy leader's time. Several years ago, I met a fierce female producer Paula Wagner who I immensely respected. I was in complete awe of her work and her charming personality. We met at an after-party of the premier of "Marshall," a film she produced, directed by Reginald Hudlin. The screening happened here in Chicago. Although I am very close friends with the director, I did not ask him to introduce us. I introduced myself to her.

Sometimes, based upon the risk you take, the other person acknowledges your bravery with a conversation. This was the case. There are times where someone may not be as nice and snub you. We've seen this in movies where the person pretends not to see you and walks away. Mrs. Wagner was gracious. I could tell immediately that she respected my grace and assertiveness. We had a great conversation. It was real and not pretentious.

I listened to her and was focused on our conversation. I wasn't distracted by others, even by the now dearly-departed *star* Chadwick Bosman or the *full cast* of "Chicago PD," circulating around the room. I was pleasantly captivated by Wagner. She took me over to her table and introduced me to her friends and husband. She told me the story of this historical feature narrative script. There was something about it that made her say *yes*. We continued to talk. She asked me about what I do for a living which offered a perfect open door for me to ask for mentoring support.

This is where learning to listen to yourself and trust your instincts comes in handy. I told her that I was an emerging producer and would love to learn how she grew her company. Having produced "Mission Impossible" with Tom Cruise and many other notable films, her eyes widened, and she grinned at the flattery. To my surprise and hers, I asked if she would be willing to mentor me. She replied, *"Now, how would that work? You live here, and I live in Los Angeles."* I assured her that I would be willing to figure that out.

Even if it meant making trips to shadow her or simply setting a monthly conference call, I shared that I would be grateful to have her mentoring support. She said okay, and gave me her email right then. From that point forward we had several mentoring sessions where she shared a number of invaluable lessons. For that support, I thanked her profusely.

In fact, her production name is a unique name. When I asked her, she said she chose it because it was intangible yet symbolic to her. However, it wasn't something that anyone could attach an image or experience to. Later I had a meaningful conversation with a marketing advisor in my circle of success. He confirmed that her advice was solid. He also endorsed my new business name. I named my production company Redwood Cove for that reason.

The most important thing to note about locating a mentor is that you never know who you will meet. You also never know who *they know*. Take the example here. My dear friend of 28 years who directed this film was very close with this producer. Therefore my new budding relationship had a meaningful relationship with my director friend. Yet did I ask my friend a lot about her or infringe on his relationship with her? No. This relates back to Chapter 1 about building *exchanging, two-sided* versus *one-sided* relationships.

Always connect and build your relationships with a focus on building a vibrant exchange of support. I respect our friendship of over 28 years. Why would I potentially jeopardize our friendship by potentially making him feel uncomfortable with unreasonable demands regarding a working relationship he has with this producer?

It's important to manage your mentoring relationships with great care and maturity. Especially if you secure a mentorship with high-profile individuals, make sure you keep the relationship confidential. I learned this lesson the hard way when I had the opportunity to be mentored by a multi-championship-winning CEO of a sports team. At the time I was running my non-profit, Smarty Pants Are Leaders, and this mentor graciously agreed to become an advisor for funding opportunities. He also helped me understand the importance of developing sound leadership skills and how to accelerate success by shifting my mindset to focus on solutions versus problems. I was so happy with this mentoring relationship until I made the mistake of breaking the unspoken confidentiality it required.

It was one night when a boyfriend I was dating, invited me to cocktails with his best friend who also happened to be a CEO of another sports team. Out of ignorance, I made mention of a conversation I had with my mentor, and before I knew it, my date's best friend made the assumption that my mentor had a different agenda. This news got back to my mentor, and it almost ruined our relationship.

I thought I could trust the person whom I was dating at the time, but I take responsibility for my error. I should not have broken a confidential relationship.

My gut never gave me the feeling that my mentor had any ill intentions. I met with him and thoroughly apologized for my error, and we agreed that, from that point forward, our mentorship would be confidential. But it was never quite the same. So if a public figure opens the doors to their world to you and is willing to share their secret sauce, respect it and, most of all, protect it.

#9 MAGICAL MANIFESTING

At the heart of creativity, I believe, is manifesting. I also believe that manifesting comes with magic baked inside it. This magical center is what gives you those flashes of inspiration that often germinate into creativity. From this vantage point, you *own* a path to a creative future filled with unique and powerful creations.

To get started on your manifestation journey to a creative life, I introduce you to a definition of creativity that I really resonate with and hope you will too, by Conchita Leeflang, Founder of Eye Am Conchita & Inventor of the Lash-App:

"When you get creative, you sleep, eat, dream your next success story. Inventions are made from creative minds who have no limits. We know what we need. We create."

So by definition alone, I'm willing to take a stand and say that out of all of the business sectors, "Creative" Entrepreneurs are possibly the most imaginative. Therefore due to their *super-power* called "Creativity," they have even more of an ability to manifest anything that they can imagine.

There are many books on visualization, manifestation, list-making, vision board directions, meditation, and all of the esoteric practices that help sharpen your creative tools. We all have what we need. It's just about remembering or tapping into our natural resources.

When I was a child, I once drew a house and colored it. It happened to be at a time when my mom was planning for us to move and was looking for a new house. One day, we drove up to the house with a tree in front on the right side that was very similar to my drawing. Ask her. She will tell you to this day that I drew the house that magically manifested. We moved into this lovely home, which became the home of many memories during high school.

As an adult, I was living in New York and having the hardest time finding a new apartment. I had been looking everywhere in Manhattan. East Side, West Side, Lower East Side... there was nothing. One day, I decided to draw an apartment and list all of the very specific amenities I wanted. I put the drawing away in a book and forgot about it. Just when I was considering leaving New York several weeks later, I got a call from a friend of mine living in Florida.

A friend of hers had an apartment in Harlem that they wanted to rent. I went up to see it and fell in love with the top floor flat with the arched windows and hardwood floors. It faced North with a sun-filled bedroom facing south. I signed a lease and moved in. A couple of months later, I recalled my drawing and went to the book only to find that the apartment was what I drew. It even had the lovely arched hallway entrance into the living room with arched windows. Unbelievable. Yet, believe.

It's not complicated. It's been said that it is by feeling the joy of your vision that magic happens. As Chopra said, once you put it into the Universe, let go of the outcome. Arguably, I would say the challenge is detaching from the outcome.

To make your Magical Manifesting List:

- State what you want, not what you do not want.
- Be Specific
- Keep it Positive
- Visualize
- Feel the joy as if it is real
- Keep it private
- Draw or cut out of a magazine

Once complete, put your list in a private place. Go about your life, and every now and then, it's okay to rejoice in the good feeling of what you want. This is faith. Now, as I have evolved just a little bit more, I also add "for my highest good." It feels really good when your vision comes true. In most cases, it is always granted in a more grand way than you would ever imagine.

#10 INTROVERT-EXTROVERT

Have you watched an interview with a famous actor who explains that in real life they are extremely shy? People always find this contrary to the persona they expect from their on-camera presence. But here's the thing: Acting, just like any other profession, is a job and requires, in most cases, years of skills and study.

A lot of creatives would describe themselves as introverts or intro/extro. I did not take a poll to state this claim. However, after over 28 years in the creative sector, I have had a lot of conversations to know this to be true. In fact, yours truly is extremely shy. Now, if you have had the pleasure of meeting me in person *(I'm really nice), I can command the attention of a thousand people in an audience. But one-on-one, uh... yeah, it can get awkward.

As a youngin, I was awkward and remarkably shy. My mother noticed this early. In the 4th grade, she put me in the Marin Theatre Company in Mill Valley, CA, in order to help me break out of my shell. In that program, I learned how to look people in the eyes using fun games like waiting to see who blinked first and trust/fall back games. She later put me in a modeling class, Dorthy Van Nuys modeling, just north of our home in San Rafael. I share all of this with you to let you know that I have learned tools that have propelled me into being an EXTROVERT when needed.

Every time I speak professionally, I establish my talk; then, before the end, I ask how many people would identify as shy? Then I tell everyone my story. Every single time, whether it's a child or an adult, they come up to me afterward, and we speak. I always encourage them that wonderful thing happen when they find a way to use their voice.

I'll always remember Precious. She came up to me after my workshop and *shared in a whisper* that she was shy. Precious is a young lady that I have seen on multiple occasions at different stages in her life. I first met her when she attended Gary Comer School. I then met her again when she was a part of a Free Spirit Media program in high school, where I lectured one summer. Just this summer, she was assigned as an Intern for a partner organization through Free Spirit and has since graduated from college.

She has become a stunning example of a person who harnessed her extrovert and let herself shine through. I have been lucky to experience her evolution. Who knows what great success she will reach? But for now, she is definitely making her way in production!

As an entrepreneur, harnessing the extrovert hiding within is a necessity. The very nature of creating a company requires that you have the ability to communicate. The sooner that you can develop your gregarious, delightful side, the more positive an experience you will have working with people you will need to grow your business. A quick, solid tip: take an improv class! I wish I had done it years before I finally did, 20 years ago! Improv will teach you how to think on your feet!

Thinking on your feet and getting the words out at the

same time is not always the easiest to do for us, shy folks. I have noticed as I have gotten older, my mind moves faster than I can get my words out. Has this ever happened to you? It's weird; sometimes, I hear myself stutter. Here's what I do: I ask my listener to give me a moment. People can be so impatient. Don't let them be. Say, "Give me a moment." And then I take my time and get the thought out.

One other trick is to develop your elevator pitch. Have a one-line description of who you are and what you do. Also, have a question that will engage the other person. This will also make it easier to engage with people when you are faced with mingling in a "Relationship Building" (formally called Networking) event.

For example, I say, "I build spaces for creatives to play on stage and or in front of a camera." This usually sparks a question and isn't what they usually hear. Instead of asking, "What do you do?" I ask, "*What keeps you busy during the day?*" Now you have a fun conversation that will be remembered by you and the listener.

#11 SHARING YOUR IDEAS: IDENTIFYING YOUR SECRETS KEEPER

How well can you hold water? It's an old saying that, if you can't hold water, it means you can't hold a secret. One thing that my mother always taught me since I was very young is this: When you are making a decision to make a change, keep it to yourself until you do so. It might seem counterintuitive, as you may feel that the more people you share your idea, the more support you will garner. However, there is something to be said about moving quietly.

In the creative sector, you may be only as successful as your idea is unique. We have many ways to secure our ideas. Writers can secure their Intellectual Property "IP" with the Writers Guild of America, Singer/songwriters register with Publishing companies. There are Patent attorneys that register your idea to protect it, and then there's the old copyright advice to send it back to yourself sealed and stamped. Do not open it! But if you have ideas like the project I am working on right now, there is no one that can protect the idea.

However, depending on the idea and the high stakes involved, you may need to identify your trusted secret keeper. This is an individual you trust and who you request to sign a

Non-Disclosure Agreement, or "NDA." For all other ideas that may or may not be able to be registered, NDAs will work to keep others from discussing your idea.

The goal is to share your idea with as few people as possible before going public. I have a series of advisors. Consider divulging only to people who have the following:

- Your best interests at heart
- The ability to invest or introduce you to investors
- Law degree, your attorney
- A stakeholder

Secret Keeper must-haves:

- Integrity
- Wisdom/ Professional Insights
- Can hold water, keep your confidence
- Track record of success

You may ask, why does the secret keeper need to have a track record of success? When you have a vision, not everyone will be able to relate let alone understand your determination. If an individual has had success they can share best practices with you.

Much like in Chapter 6, it's important for you to determine if your idea has market appeal. I advise you to speak with someone who you trust to tell you the truth. There is also a Non-Compete Agreement that you can have signed by industry professionals who may have shared interests.

Lastly, if you believe in energy and/or physics, there is the idea that it's best to keep the energy tight, thereby it remains powerful as opposed to spreading it thin, reducing the power for it to manifest. You get to decide.

#12: KEEPING QUIET

Shhhhhhhh...

Keeping quiet may be one of the most challenging things to do when you have a great idea. You will have friends that you will want to tell. Don't. You may have a side hustle and want to tell your co-workers about your future company idea. Don't. Zip it!

If you have not already started a journal, I suggest you create an ideas journal. This will help you channel some of your excitement down on paper. This will also provide a document of your progress that you can review later.

You may want to post on social media. Don't. I am always torn by the idea of creating grassroots marketing by sharing what's to come on social media. We all see how "influencers" develop followers. Corporations, the music business, fashion and every other industry now gauge their interests in your company based on the number of followers you have. But it's up to you to know your creative business and when to share your ideas. But until that time. Keep it tight. Keep quiet. Save the Loud for your Launch!

Shhhhhhhhhhhhh... Shhhhhhtttt..... Shhhhhhhhpppp!

#13: CHOOSING THE OPPORTUNITY

So, many ideas flood your mind. How do you choose the right opportunity? Creative entrepreneurs have the ability to create all of the time. In fact, it is evident that once you have one outlet, like music, fashion and design, other vertices follow. Producers may have several projects in their slate, on their virtual plate, while the project you think is the least likely to succeed may be the top performer.

Sometimes the opportunity chooses you. Several years ago here in Chicago I was a member of 1871, the largest tech incubator in the world. I, along with Howard Tillman and a select few were invited to go listen to Sir Richard Branson speak at McCormick Place.

One thing that I will always remember is that Sir Richard Branson spoke of the time he created Virgin Airlines. This was an opportunity that one could say chose him. He explained that he had a very important date to get to in the Virgin Islands. In fact, he did not want to be late and there he was, sitting on the tarmac in a delayed flight.

The plane was having technical difficulties and taxied back to the gate. At that point, he went to the airline and said, "I would like to buy a plane." They said, "Well, sir, you can't just buy a plane." He replied, "Then I need to speak with a manager because I need to get to the Virgin Islands, and I cannot be late." I don't recall the name of the airline, but they put him on the phone with the manufacturer. He assured them that he would pay with his American Express card. Based on who he was and his reputation, they agreed to allow him to buy one plane.

They further explained to him that they didn't sell planes alone, but that he would need to buy an entire fleet. He informed them that he would consider this overnight, and based upon how the plane flew to the Virgin Islands, he would get back to them regarding whether or not he would invest in more planes the next day. So once he bought the plane, he went back to the other passengers and offered to fly them to the Virgin Islands for a reduced rate.

He packed the plane and made his date on time. Can you imagine who his date was? His current wife to this day. It was their first date. He explained that LOVE was the motivation for him creating Virgin Airlines. And in this case, the opportunity chose him.

One could say that he took advantage of the situation and was afforded an incredible opportunity.I was fortunate enough to be sitting in the front row. After his talk, he came down into the audience and for some reason I threw my hands in the air as if to welcome and embrace him, and he hugged me. I was told by our team that there was a photo. It was real. He was respectful and genuine. It was very kind. And I felt seen.

And yet another great opportunity came as I was able to share my genuine gratitude with a hug. Now he has flown to the outer layer of earth, call it space! Greg W. Reid, Health Tech Innovator and Founder of the company, Calibrated has this to say about choosing the opportunity:

"I will never forget a chance encounter I had with a television producer from the *Star Trek* TV series (the most recent ones). At the time, I was writing for television, and I whimsically asked him the secret of his success, after some small talk at a coffee shop.

What he told me offered a new perspective on making choices in business and in life. He said, "We will always be in a process to evaluate our opportunities in life, and choosing them wisely actually is an art form.

As he sipped his brew, he peeked up to make sure I was listening, and I was. He went on, "It's very simple. Your chosen opportunity has to be aligned with the things that you can execute better than anyone else so that you honor its potential. It's not just that a door is open for you to walk through.

Your first step into that chosen opportunity must have the intention that you will honor it with talents and resources that no one else can offer it. With that top of mind, you can never fail."

I gratefully thanked him, of course. Then as he was ready to exit the café I asked, "Can I open the door for you?" He winked at me knowingly and replied, "Is that all you got?"

#14: WORTHWHILE RISKS

Let's level-set for a moment here. When I say "risk averse," what does that mean to you? When I say "risk tolerance," what does that mean to you? It is absolutely okay if neither of these terms resonates with you because generally, they are used by venture capitalist investors, angel investors, portfolio managers, family offices, and others of the like.

Simply put, risk-averse equates to a "no." As defined by the dictionary: "risk averse: disinclined or reluctant to take risks." In other words, you ask someone to invest in your company or idea, and they say no.

Risk tolerance is defined as the degree of variability in investment returns that an investor is willing to withstand in their financial planning. Simply put, how much of someone else's money or your money that you are willing to risk without knowing if there's a return on that investment. How much money are you or someone else willing to lose? Do you have money to lose?

There's the risk that you're willing to take by virtue of creating a company and the worthwhile risks that others are willing to invest in your risk/business.

I have not taken a poll because most people are fatigued with online polls. But I am willing to bet that most entrepreneurs—keywords: *most entrepreneurs* are not considering the development of their business as a risk. Sure, it can be risky. However, we are all risk-takers. And *most entrepreneurs do not have money to lose*!

There's a difference in the risk that we are willing to take when we are creating our vision and implementing it into a real business versus the type of risks that I asked you about at the beginning of this chapter. Risk-averse and risk tolerance are not RISKS that most small creative business owners are consciously aware of taking. Yet to know this language is to better understand the BUSINESS OF YOUR BUSINESS. (More about this in Chapter 18)

At the top of 2021, it became very clear to me that as access to capital flies open to historically marginalized communities of color, otherwise described as BIPOC Communities, there's not only historically been a gap in resources but also a language barrier. The language of business is like any other sector in that there are specific terms that relate to very specific outcomes.

I think it's important that individuals have a greater understanding of these types of terms, so they are not operating in the dark. No one wants to feel like someone is talking over their heads. Business owners want to feel prepared. Individuals want to have the right tools to generate success. So while I was the director for the Center for Creative Entrepreneurship, it became apparent that before we do any education event planning for the year, it was important to create a Resource Roundtable. Due to the pandemic, unfortunately, we were not able to hold an in-person Town Hall. But I wanted this to be equally as impactful.

I wanted people to feel seen and heard by other entrepreneurs who look like them and by individual stakeholders who could help serve their needs. This initiative was to speak to real people in disinvested communities about disparities that they experienced; blind spots, gaps in resources, barriers to entry, or simply how they felt going into a bank and asking for a loan. What were their experiences? By doing so, the intention was to make sure that these business owners had the resources that they needed, and if not, we provided guidance for them so that they have the tools enabling their success.

One glaring outcome was that business owners didn't always understand the language of investors. Do you know the difference between a Family Office and an Angel Investor? Why would an individual who does not have the risk tolerance of $10,000 understand what a family office is? A family office is a business that has been created in the name of a WEALTHY family to invest or donate funds. As defined: Family offices are private wealth management advisory firms that serve ultra-high-net-worth individuals.

The point I am trying to make is that assumptions should never be made. Unless a creative entrepreneur has gone to Business School, which is seldom the case, and has learned the language of business, people who are in the business of offering services to those who are underserved must first find out what the needs are by asking the individuals. In most cases, the emerging business owner may not know the "language of the business" or what to ask for.

Okay, so now that I have given a distinction between risks and worthwhile risks, let's get down to the RISK that we all take when launching a business. At this point, you've determined whether or not your idea has a market value. Is it "Sticky"? Is your vision valuable? If you can say yes to these questions... JUMP! I once had a friend say to me, "Saudia,

JUMP!... Take the risk. What's the worst that can happen? You will always be good at sales, and someone will always hire you."

So I encourage you... Take the leap!

#15: HOW TO MAKE IT SAUCY

In today's tech-enabled and social media conscious world, you gotta make it "Saucy". As a follow-on to in Chapter #6, "Sticky: Is Your Vision Valuable, making it saucy is how to make it **stick** in your brain! Marketing is one thing, but having a strategic plan in marketing with conscious intention is something altogether totally different.

That means understanding who your market is and what's going to best attract their attention. You can have a great idea, but if you're not putting it into perspective, in the market for which it's meant, then it could get missed or you just might not get as much traction. Making it saucy is making it sexy. Think outside of what's expected. Instead of using a static graphic, consider using a motion graphic. Keep it simple but catchy.

Translate your vision into short bite-sized taglines that fit on an Instagram post, and on Facebook or Twitter. Research has been done to confirm that facial recognition or photos really grab more likes or clicks. So you ask, "Why do clicks matter?" They do. Especially in the music industry, film industry and fashion industry, people want to see how many people are following your idea because in their databases with thousands spent on research, somehow that translates to dollars.

One music industry veteran explained that some music executives do not even listen to the talent they are courting, but rather they look at their social media numbers, which now guide their decision. In some cases the talent does NOT have talent. There is something to be said about making it SAUCY, but also having talent. For those singers out there who can REALLY SING, this can be a sad thing, because the people who are better at marketing themselves are getting more traction. I do not endorse shallow, phony, opportunistic business ideas. Over time I believe that TRUE talent will sustain a business after the flare of social media fans fade.

#16: CIRCLE OF SUCCESS

We all know the sayings: *"Be careful of the company you keep,"* or *"Lay down with dogs and wake up with fleas."* Well, the latter is more along the lines of dating... As my dear Granddaddy would favorably say, *"You get the picture!"*

Here's another one: *"Keep your friends close and your enemies closer."* One, I do my best not to create enemies, and two, I choose to keep closest to me the people I love and respect. So generally, I do not accept this old saying. In fact, in *keeping my house clean,* as I refer to in Chapter 25, this also relates to people. Why would you keep people that you know do not like you, or have your best interest in mind, around? It doesn't make sense to me.

You do what you wish. Some people consider social capital only by numbers. I do not. But I also believe in building relationships, not networking. In her book *Networking is Dead: Making Connections That Matter*, Melissa G Wilson and her coauthor Larry Mohl describe networking as being like seeing how many numbers you can gain by the end of the night. It resembles social media numbers without substance. How many people do you actually know or have had meaningful conversations with on LinkedIn? I like to pride myself on the fact that I can safely say at this point, I know 97% of my LinkedIn connections.

Your circle of success includes your family, friends, fans, partners, mentors, mentees, assistants, secret keepers, investors, marketing team, advisors, strategic partners, and all of the people that provide the solid foundation for which you will build your vision.

Your circle of success can also be the space in which you operate. Consider that your environment has a direct effect on your ability to function optimally.

Your circle of success can also be the organizations or foundations that support you and your vision. I recently won a grant that will provide not only some financial support to move my current development forward but will also provide educational tools to ensure my company's success. The entire foundation is a part of my circle of success.

Once you identify your circle of success, give thanks and feel free to share with those who are in your circle of success that they are, in fact, a part of the circle. This will reinforce their commitment and provide them with your acknowledgment of their support.

#17: WHEN IT FEELS LIKE IT'S GOING WRONG...

It is! Because at this point, you have learned how to listen to yourself and trust your inner compass. But maybe it isn't going wrong. It isn't, because you have enough faith and wherewithal to make it *right*! Others may doubt you or try to talk you out of what you know is right. You must keep in mind that your vision was a gift to you for a reason.

Keep in mind the *reason,* or problem that you are meant to solve. In Eastern Buddhist philosophy, this *truth/reason* or your Life's Mission, is referred to as Dharma.

In Indian religion, the eternal and inherent nature of reality is regarded in Hinduism as a cosmic law underlying right behavior and social order:

- (in Buddhism) the nature of reality is regarded as a universal truth taught by the Buddha; the teaching of Buddhism.
- an aspect of truth or reality.

In this book I reference many cultures and various philosophies because I believe we can learn from everyone. Yet I have always been encouraged to look within, and I encourage you to do the same. You must learn how to listen to your gut. Check in with yourself because, ultimately, you know when something is right and when it is wrong.

Oftentimes, the journey of the entrepreneur is a lonely one. You may have an idea that is so far advanced that either no one believes you, or they simply cannot wrap their head around your idea. In some cases, women are marginalized because their male counterparts just can't believe that she figured such a thing out.

Or it could be an investor who doesn't trust or believe that a Black or Latinx person has the capacity to sustain the business for a return on the investment/ROI. These are real occurrences not to be dismissed, yet also not to be adopted as an excuse. You don't want to walk around with a chip on your shoulder. No one will want to work with you; not because of your gender or your race, but because of a poor attitude.

Then there is time. Time and the universal flow doesn't always align with our brain or our master plan. Like an express train moving full steam ahead, taking turns effortlessly and only coming to a halt to begin making all local stops. We may believe that everything is on track, and when things stop or there is a significant pause, you may question if something's going wrong.

This is when taking a moment to reflect and reassess is required. Sometimes we are given this space to circle back and make sure all is in order so that as we move forward, we are more clearly set up for success.

Here's more wisdom from Genevieve Thiers, Tech Innovator and Founder of Sitter City:

> I remember there was a period in the company when we had a lot of young talent turning over. It was right after we had started our initial team... We were about 12 or 13 people.

Suddenly about half the team ended up having life changes and we were down to a skeleton crew. It was terrifying. But it was also the best thing that could've happened because I really needed industry experts to come in at that point for the C level roles. I found them and we continued stronger than ever.

#18 LEARNING TO JUGGLE: THE BUSINESS OF YOUR BUSINESS

Juggling is fun. It feels risky and provides excitement both from the spectator and the juggler. Don't worry. You don't have ADHD or Attention Deficit Disorder. Most entrepreneurs have the ability to multitask beyond what others consider normal. It's part of what makes us successful. We have the ability to think about more than one thing at a time and to ideate and create more businesses simultaneously. Most people can't wrap their heads around that.

Now, if you don't know how to multitask or think about multiple things at the same time, here's a good reason to learn how: Learning how to juggle is also learning how to balance. Balance is one of the most important factors in our lives.

Juggling is not the same as Skatterization. The ability to juggle well would suggest a sophisticated level of organization. In fact, I will step out on a limb and say that juggling is a form of brain balance. Keeping all of the balls in the air requires hand/eye coordination as well as a steadiness. Stepping away from the metaphor and entering the realm of the real world in business, the same kind of coordination as described as juggling, is generally a learned skill in business.

The fortunate or unfortunate part is that this skill is generally learned by trial and error, by doing. I am not sure that there is a course out there for entrepreneurs on how to multitask successfully. Looking for efficiencies and time management are essential elements for multitasking.

Looking for efficiencies relates to what some now refer to as "life hacks." For instance, instead of walking down the street to the end of the corner and crossing at the crosswalk that's in an L formation, one might cross at a diagonal and bypass the crosswalk.

I'm not saying that it's okay to cut corners in business. However, when walking I do cut corners, and when driving, I will take a diagonal street when it's an option. It's more about where you can alleviate time spent in order to have more time in other places.

I share this example because it's a way to define the different choices that some people make in every aspect of their life. Maybe I refined this practice living in Manhattan in the backseat of a taxi. I am that person who directs the taxi to arrive at my destination in the most time-efficient and cost-effective way.

Not all entrepreneurs have a multiplicity mind set. I happen to identify as a multihyphenate. Some creatives are singularly focused. There is no judgment either way.

Knowing how you do business helps you better understand the *business* of your *business*. This is not to be taken for granted. Just because you have a great idea that has a market demand, and you know you are on the right track, does not mean that you absolutely know how to run the business of your business. You may need to identify a partner who is more suited than you. In fact, in Chapter 21, "How to Discern a Good Partner," I get into more specific details.

I will use myself as an example. I have been in the film/tv

business for over 28 years. I know some aspects of the business that I have focused on. I am a successful producer for that reason. But I do not know *every* aspect, such as the basics of the Art Department or how to score music. I know how to choose a track that best suits the visual and yet, I do not score films. Although I have developed a thousand-seat theatre auditorium that was vacant and gutted for 45 years, I am not an architect.

And although I want to build a film studio, I had no idea that the rentals of a space include charging for trash and WiFi. Huh? Yep! But when you are operating a business, you absolutely need to understand margins and the difference between the money that is "earned revenue" and every cost that impacts your bottom line. A scheduled script budget is the best way to see the breakdown of cost associated with the end project. In other businesses, this may be a pro-forma budget.

When we watch a movie, we are simply enjoying the movie. We do not consider how many blue-and-white striped shirts were purchased for that one scene that had two takes in two days. We do not consider that for a dinner setting where the actor throws a wine glass into the fireplace that there are ten duplicates of the same glass placed for every take. Each glass has an associated cost.

Or when we listen to a great song, we do not consider how much studio time was rented or how many times the song was mixed to achieve what we now hear streaming. Knowing the business while juggling the costs, the margins, and the net value associated with your business will save you and sustain you at the same time. Again from Conchita Leeflang Founder of Eye Am Conchita & Inventor of the Lash-App comes this insight:

> The ability to keep three objects (balls) in the air at the same time proves that being a mother, business woman and wife

should be an easy task once we know how to focus without distraction.

#19: HOW TO PICK UP THE PIECES

So after juggling and dropping a couple of balls, you understand that you do not have a lot of capacity to continue without it costing you. Sometimes while juggling, we can lose our focus, when this happens, things are destined to fall through the proverbial cracks. How do you recover, pick up the proverbial pisces and keep moving forward?

This is a time to take a moment. Take a breath. It might even be worth taking a bit of a vacation to a quiet location to rest and reassess in order to holistically recover. This is not a time to take a vacation with family or friends. When there is a fissure or a "glitch" in The Matrix, it's time to discover the problem. This is the time to fix it or change course. Because when a fissure is not sealed, the splinter continues to grow into a larger crack and eventually it will break.

Often, this is the universe's way of slowing you down to take a moment to determine if you are on the right track. Just because you have a great idea, and all roads are leading to what appears to be success, you may actually be veering away from your life's path. That's if you believe that you have a path.

If you cannot afford the time or expense to break away to a quiet retreat, find a quiet room and ground yourself regularly. Then once at home, set a time to be quiet and meditate or isolate yourself so that you can hear your thoughts. On second thought, under these circumstances, I would listen less to your thoughts, which might be overflowing, and listen more to your heart. Does that make sense?

Take a moment to not listen to all of the thoughts, but rather focus on quieting the mind. Listen to your own breath, put your less dominant hand on your heart, and ask yourself, "What should I do? What is best for my highest good?" You will get an answer. The question is whether or not you will listen and take action accordingly. Charisse Conanan Johnson, Author of A Wealthy Girl: 7 Steps to Prosperity, Peace and Personal Power and Managing Partner at Next Street has the following story to share in this regard:

> I closed my fintech company that I poured my savings, soul, and sweat equity into over four years. I had to accept the reality that closing my business was indeed the best business decision. I also started working with a therapist to handle the depression that comes with feeling like you are a failure. I re-centered myself on the next chapter of my professional journey with the help of a career coach who focuses on professional transitions. I relied on my faith, or belief in a future that I could not see today, to help me pick up the broken pieces of a dream deferred.
>
> I eventually realized that while the *business* failed, *I am* still a success. I have used the lessons that I learned during my entrepreneurial journey to relaunch a successful website (www.charissesays.com) on wealth creation, write a book, and lead a 50-person firm that helps other entrepreneurs get

access to the capital, customers, and services they need to thrive. I chose to pick up the pieces of a closed business, surrounded myself with the support I needed, and positively channeled my experiences into the next chapter of my life."

#20: IDENTIFYING INVESTORS

It's extremely important that you are clear about what you are doing and that you have done your due diligence before bringing anyone to the table to financially back your vision. Any VC, Angel Investor, or foundation, for that matter, will expect that you already have a business plan. And in some cases, they would expect that you have already beta tested your model. Always consider the other person's time. You don't want to waste it.

The last thing you want to do is ruin a relationship because you have not done your research. Identifying investors can be as simple or as complicated as you want it to be. Like anything, the more experience you have, relatively speaking, the easier things can be... maybe.

First, I would suggest you consider your circle of success. Who are the individuals within that circle who already believe in you? People invest in people, not necessarily the idea. What I mean by that is that although you may have a grand idea, investors are looking at the idea for sure, but they are mostly considering Who You Are and how capable you are of achieving that great idea.

Your integrity, your reputation, your history of achievement, how you treat people, and who you are associated with, or "the relationships that you keep" ultimately tells the story of whether or not you can be taken seriously and can be trusted with this investor's dollars.

Now, something to consider that is not an intuitive thought is that once you have earned an investor's trust and therefore they are willing to invest... you become the protector of their investment. Maybe it's just me, but I protect the hell out of their money! Why? Because here again, this is another type of relationship that is developing. The success of this investment will yield more future investments. I'm not a one-and-done kind of person. I'm more interested in the long-term gains. Investor relationship building generally takes time.

There are unique opportunities, however, where you may have an idea about which a particular investor has interests. Having done your research and diligence before setting up the meeting, you were able to determine that the interest is already aligned with the investor, which makes for a faster decision.

You may have walked into a situation where you have the idea for which they were already interested in investing. I was extremely fortunate that this happened to me recently. I identified four developers that I wanted to work with. I deepened my research around each one and their respective companies. Although I had begun to set up meetings, one company, in particular, I found aligned even closer with my vision.

Here's where your relationships are resources. I happened to know at least five people who had a relationship with this particular founder. I decided to have a particular person who is an expert in the prospective business make the introduction to the founder and company. Why did I choose the expert over a friend who used to work for the founder? One might think that the closer person to the founder might be the right connection. But flip it around. By having the expert make the introduction on my behalf, that introduction works in my favor as it also becomes an endorsement of his belief in my ability.

A lot of creative entrepreneurs and small business entrepreneurs do not always think about reaching for outside investment into their company. This may be because of a lack of understanding of how outside capital can help grow your company. I had a friend say to me that she wouldn't want outside investment because it would take more of her money. I had to stop her and ask, what do you mean? And she said, "Well, if somebody invests in my company, then for the money that I make, they're going to take more money out. And then I mentioned the TV show *Shark Tank* and asked her, "Have you ever watched it?"

She replied, "Yeah." I responded, "Well, much like on the show, every deal that is drawn up into a contract is different." It's in the best interest of the investor for you to make as much money as possible because they get a percentage of your earnings. But it's not that they make more money from you. It's more that you have more ability to make more money, and then you agree to the terms of the percentage that they take."

She said, "Wow! Yeah, I guess you're right." And it flipped her mindset. It all goes back to not a lot of people really understanding the business of the business. So it's absolutely imperative that you understand your business and what you want to achieve with your business.

Not every company requires an outside investor. And not all investors are interested in Creative Entrepreneur businesses. Figure out what works best for you and for your sustainable success. I have said that success is defined by the person. You may be happy with a company that allows you to pay yourself, buy a house, pay your mortgage, pay a child's tuition, go on several vacations a year, and live life with less stress. That may be enough. I define that person as "the door."

They do their work to get shit done, and they have a happy life. Not everybody is searching for fame. Not everyone wants to be famous. Not everyone wants to exit out of a company at a quarter of a billion dollars. However, if you have a company that aligns well with outside capital, then be sure to identify the right investor for your business. Rely on your advisors and your circle of success to help when you are determining the best fit. Nick Moran, Founder of New Stack Ventures, has this story to share:

> "When I first began raising capital, I struggled to find the right investors. I went to conferences, wrote cold emails, joined groups on LinkedIn and yet still could not get any momentum. On a particularly frustrating day, I met a friend for lunch. She asked how I was doing and I explained the challenge of finding the right investors for my fund.
>
> She then asked me for more information on the type of person I was looking for. Once I explained the profile, she suggested a couple of people in her network who might have an interest and offered to share the details of my fund.
>
> It was then that I realized that I had built a valuable network of friends and allies over many years. These people want to help; they just don't know how. The search for investors doesn't begin on the internet or at a conference, it begins with the people that you've built trust and credibility with. Trust is transferable. A great referral significantly increases the odds of a successful pitch. Once I shared our goals with my close network and asked for their help, the fundraiser gained momentum and we closed a larger fund than originally planned."

#21: HOW TO DISCERN A GOOD PARTNER

I have always been someone who takes people at their word. If you tell me you're going to do something, I believe you. In fact, as a child, it wasn't fun because people would make jokes all the time, and I would just believe them, and they would say, "Saudia, we're kidding." To this day, I choose to maintain a certain level of that kind of innocence because it helps me determine and decipher whether or not people are true to their word.

When looking for a good partner, you need to be able to trust that person. Trust. Trust. Trust. But before you can trust anyone, you have to get to know them a little bit. Or, at the very least, know someone who knows them well and can vouch for their integrity.

How do you define a partner? Is this a business partner that shares equity in a business with you? Are they strategic partners who have a business that complements your business? In this chapter, I am referring to the kind of business partner with whom you share some aspect of your business.

I am going to share with you another Richard Branson story because it literally freed me up. During the SAGE conference that I mentioned earlier, where I had the joy of meeting Sir Richard Branson, he said something that changed the course of how I do business.

It was something to the effect of When you are a visionary, a person who creates a vision for which a business is launched. It's imperative that you find a partner who can execute that vision. He went on to say add something like This person or partner needs to be so aligned with how you think that it's almost as if they are in your head. They have the capacity to understand you and how you think. Before you can finish the sentence, they've already finished it for you.

Branson continued, When you can find this person, this will free you up to continue to create. The more freedom you have to create, the more businesses that you can manifest. Not every creative has the ability to execute their brilliant idea. So find someone brilliant to put your vision into action so that you can continue to create.

Wow! All of the pressure that I put on myself for so many years trying to figure out things that were difficult for me would, at times, distract me away from the process of the business that I wanted to create. For many years, I hid that I was dyslexic. I would only take jobs that would allow me to do great work without exposing what, at the time, I felt was a major disability.

Just taking time to figure out an Excel spreadsheet, which is totally not my thing, would get me so frustrated it was all but paralyzing. Thankfully, when I moved to Chicago with Smith and Hawken, I had a regional director with whom I shared my dyslexia. He said, "Oh, that's not a problem. We just won't have you do the scheduling on an Excel spreadsheet." He didn't make as big of a deal out of it as I thought anybody would, and from that point forward, I stopped hiding my dyslexia.

As one who does not like to be boxed in by labels, even

putting it down in this book makes me a bit nervous. I don't want to be defined by it. I've lived my whole life overachieving so that nobody would see it. So once Branson shared this wisdom, it literally freed me up to think differently, and I immediately started considering who could be that partner.

I didn't find my partner right away. It took a couple of years. First, we became friends. As I got to know what she did, I hired her for a couple of productions. I guess I was unconsciously providing work interviews. Then one day, she and her husband asked if I would help them produce a short film. I said yes. But while I was working for her, I experienced her level of efficiency and detail-oriented precision. Wow! I was beyond impressed.

I am a detail-driven person with a slight touch of undiagnosed OCD. Not really, but it would seem so. Anyway, the level of integrity in her production paperwork and organization caught my attention.

I am not selfish, but I am selfish. When another executive asked me if I knew anyone that could become her assistant, I immediately recommended this individual. I said, "She is the only person that I know like me, and I would risk my reputation on it because she is reliable, and if you need her, she is there!" The executive did not hire her. Oh, well. I ended up hiring her myself.

To this day, I refer to my dear friend and partner Kayla Jones as my right arm. She understands me and has seen me through both success and not-so-easy situations. She never raises her voice; she has a calm demeanor even when I know she is upset. She is a balance to my personality. This book is probably the only thing I have not asked her to work with me on lately. She is what Sir Richard Branson described as "finding the right fit."

While she has her own production company, our skills in

what we do are dissimilar enough that we are often able to work with one another, for one another, or refer each other out for other jobs. With my upcoming major development, of course, I asked her to consider coming on board. She's a keeper! I pray we are friends for life.

My other trusted partner and I met under a unique circumstance. I attended Sundance for the first time during the Polar Vortex winter of 2019. My flight to Chicago was canceled, and all of the hotels were booked. I met this individual at a screening of *Talk Back.* She overheard my situation and offered to let me stay in her hotel room. Little did we know that although Anastasia lives in Los Angeles, she is originally from Chicago and attended Columbia College. Wait. There's more.

That night in our double beds, like a schoolgirl slumber party, we figured out that we share the same Entertainment Attorney, Tom Leavens. Wow! We were fast friends. Her flight was departing the next morning back to L.A. super early. I was due to have breakfast and see a movie with Tom. Sure enough, he laughed and could believe how Anastasia and I met. To this day, she is the *truth, one of the truest people I know,* working on productions, and what I like to refer to as my left arm! I have also invited her to work with me on my major development. That's if Disney does not lock her down first! Time is of the essence.

My last example is slightly different but basically the same. I spoke of this person in the earlier chapter on Identifying Investors. This partner is an investor as well. My first reaction to our meeting was that it felt right! Of course, there was also the fact that he said yes to my request. Before that, I liked his energy and his enthusiasm about a song I played, Frank Sinatra and Count Basie's *My Kind of Town.* He told me a really great story.

This partner seemed down to earth and genuinely friendly.

To me, that's a person I want to do business with because when times get rough, and those times will happen, you want to have a relatively friendly person on your team.

Ultimately your gut and your intuition will help you discern a good partner. It can take time or can be immediate. Another business partner, a Producer, checks everything against whether the person has a good heart. That's a great way to gauge as well. Whatever way you choose to gauge it, you will know.

#22: TRUST YOUR INNER COMPASS

Are you directionally challenged? Can you read a REAL compass? Compasses, like maps, are rarely ever used these days. The iPhone still has the compass app, and I love it, but I rarely use it. It's funny. As long as I know where a body of water is and the direction in which it lies, I am good. You can drop me in the middle of a city, and I can find my way.

In Chicago, Lake Michigan is East of everything, and in California, where I grew up, the ocean is always West of everything. Now having lived in Manhattan, it was a bit different living on an island where the water was on both sides, but again, I know my East from my West.

Your inner compass, however, is that internal guidance tool that helps you navigate through life. Is yours turned on, on pause, or has it ever been activated? I wrote earlier about "Learn How to Listen" in Chapter 7. The difference here is that by now, your inner compass should be spinning for two reasons: First, you are actively participating in the exercises in this book thus far, and second, your gut is awake.

The directional needle of a compass spins until it settles on the stated direction. Now it's about you being the one to get steady and follow the direction of the arrow.

The only real way that you can screw up your creative entrepreneurship endeavors is to go counter to your intuition. Another way to state this is, you willingly and knowingly go in the opposite direction for which your inner compass is directing you. This means you do not trust yourself, or this can simply be defined as self-sabotaging your success. Some people have a very real fear of success and unknowingly sabotage their ability for greatness. For example, if you say, "I want to go north," and your inner compass is directing you north, but instead, you decide to go south...well, that's going to reflect in an immediate negative outcome.

Why create more problems for yourself than you need to? When in doubt, keep it simple. Life isn't as complicated as we all seem to make it. Part of our reason for being here is to have fun and enjoy the journey along the way. As Keon Parsons, Fine Art Appraiser Keon Parsons & Associates shares:

> "Planning is an act of faith."

#23: MANAGING FAMILY EXPECTATIONS

Managing family expectations can be challenging. While most people would consider their family as their first layer of support or early adopters of their circle of success, for this reason it can be difficult to create boundaries. Family obligations are quite different for everyone. Whether you are single, live with a partner, live with one or both parents or are married with children, finding time and space to further your business endeavors requires that you set reasonable boundaries with family members.

One thing that we hear about all of the time from entrepreneurs is that someone in their family, a parent or a spouse, couldn't understand why they spent so much time on a "side hustle" when they have a "real job." Or for those entrepreneurs who take the leap into the abyss of faith to launch a company without a 9-5, friends or family may say... "Why don't you get a REAL job?"

In Chapter 25 I speak about keeping your house clean and surrounding yourself with positive energy as opposed to negative energy. People who share this kind of concern do not realize that they are being negative, because let's face it, it's actually their way of sharing concern for you. They just do not understand. I bring this up because in a lot of cultures, for so long a 9-5 job or a career in medicine or law were the beacons of hope for marginalized communities. These kinds of jobs were billed to be a "Get out of poverty card"! But the real way to establish generational wealth building is to actually build a profitable company. I come from a strong legacy of women entrepreneurs.

As a Black Woman whose grandparents owned a lemon farm in Texas before moving to San Francisco, I come from working people! My grandmother owned two hair salons and my grandfather ("Grandaddy") worked two jobs: he was a master welder in the shipyards and did a number of things in the community. They did not understand my mother's desire to put my sister and me into private schools. They believed in working! My grandparents had five children, and each of their children had three or more children, except for my mother.

She had two: me and my sister. My sister and I are the first generation in our family to graduate from four years of college with a degree and my sister went on to become a doctor. Yes, my mother went to college at San Francisco State and studied Psychology. She was also a successful professional jazz singer early in her life before she had us.

My mother had to work while raising my sister, which delayed her ability to earn her degree. The point is, our mother traveled and she saw the world and experienced more of a fast-paced life. My dad was an entrepreneur—a master upholsterer. He was very talented, but sadly, he passed away when I was in high school. My mother wanted more for us and she made sure we had it.

We went to the best schools, Convent of the Sacred Heart on Broadway in San Francisco. In my first year of high school, my mother figured out a aspect in the medical industry that was missing. From that, she created her own company to solve the problem that she discovered. Needless to say, she was an entrepreneur and because of that, I was inspired to start early with my first company at the age of seven: Nature's Images, by Saudia. My mother provided the support of my early entrepreneurial endeavors because she understood, having taken the leap herself leaving a 9-5.

However, support of the entrepreneurial dream is usually not the case in disinvested, historically marginalized communities. Families are doing what they can to survive and pay the bills. To be an entrepreneur may seem like a luxury at the very least, and at the very most a very selfish endeavor.

I mentioned earlier that the journey for a creative entrepreneur can be a lonely one. But here are tips on how to create meaningful moments and healthy family boundaries:

1. Find a time that aligns with your family members schedule and set a weekly catch up call, dinner, or coffee. This may seem very business-like, but you want to consider that until your business reaches a level of success, YOU ARE YOUR BUSINESS. So time management is important. This will help you protect your capacity and reduce the opportunity for burnout.
2. Hard stop. This is different from your client meetings, but still creates the expectation with a start and end time. We do this for dinner parties, right? I suggest that you factor in that you will dilly-dally a bit beyond your end time. This way your personal time doesn't feel like a business meeting.
3. Consider a hobby that you like to do with your family. Make it fun and do your best to switch it up

a bit when you can. Or maybe it's gathering every Sunday for dinner.

4. Do not always talk about business and what you are up to. This gets boring and furthermore, they may not really understand what you do. Make it more about them.
5. Be attentive and present. Get your calls out of the way so that you can sit your phone down. Put an "out of office" reply to emails if you must. Be PRESENT.

By doing this you are developing meaningful memories that will sustain you and your relationship over time. Personally, I have not always been as present or attentive. I would be looking at my phone or taking a call when I was spending time with my mother. As you can imagine, she expressed that I was being selfish. At the time, I was a bit defensive at first because I was considering attending to my business. But here's the thing: When our loved ones leave us, that's time that we cannot get back. So find fun ways to share space with one another. When it's lovely out, go for a walk, grill outside, have cocoa by a fire or simply watch a show together.

#24: STAYING GROUNDED

How often do you find yourself reeling with thoughts, excitement and so energized that you can hardly sit still? Although I highly recommend this, I am not a licensed therapist. There are times in the creative process that require you to center yourself. Centering is slightly different from getting focused. One creates the space for the other.

Centering yourself allows you to get to a place in order to focus. Staying grounded is not as easy as it sounds. Yet it is very important to maintain a connection to the present moment. When we are creating, we are mostly imagining into the future. But this present moment is essential.

Imagine your ideas are like helium-filled balloons that need an anchor to keep them on the table in the room and not float up to the ceiling. Grounding is like providing yourself an anchor to keep you in the present moment. Ideas are great but at times, they can become quite lofty and unattainable. Staying "grounded" also helps you "keep it real!" as Dave Chapelle would say in his skit, *"When keeping it Real Goes Wrong"*... (That person was probably not grounded, not in touch with reality or present to the truth of the moment/situation).

Here is an exercise to stay grounded. This is a great technique to do before an important meeting. You can also try this anytime you feel like your ideas are floating all over the place.

Once you learn how to do this for yourself anytime that you feel out of sync or that you need to get connected, you will have this tool to do so.

Find a comfortable seat where you can put both of your feet on the ground. I recommend sitting up straight on a chair or sofa. For this exercise, I do not recommend lying down or sitting cross-legged. You should sit in a chair that allows for your legs to be at a 90-degree angle from the knee, with your feet flat against the floor.

Rest your hands on your knees, palms facing down. That means your hands should be resting on your knees. Take three deep breaths in through your nose with your eyes open, and release your breath through your mouth.

In the same position, now close your eyes as you take one deep breath in through your nose. Fill your belly with air. Hold your breath for 4 counts and breathe out through your mouth for 6 counts, compressing your belly. You are filling your belly (diaphragm) as if you are blowing up a balloon. Then when you release your breath, it's as if the air is coming out of the balloon. Singers, athletes, actors and practitioners of regular meditation know all about diaphragmatic breathing.

Do this again. Take a deep breath in through your nose, hold for 4, then let the breath flow out through your mouth with a count of 6. Do this 3-5 times, and then breathe normally.

Keeping your eyes closed following the same breath pattern, next imagine that your feet are like tree trunks rooted to the ground. Next you want to imagine what's just below your feet. Is it concrete? Is it a wood floor? How many floors are you up from the ground? Are you in a home on the first floor, which means there's a basement? Are you in an apartment building or high-rise office building that's 20+ floors up?

How high are you up from the solid ground? Keep this in mind and for every level you are above ground, imagine going so many levels down to get to the soil. Do this for yourself and visualize that your feet are like tree trunks rooted in the soil. Once you get to the soil, imagine what's beneath that? How far down are you willing to ground? To the core of the earth?

Get that image really clear in your mind. Keeping your hands palms down touching your knees, begin to feel your knees. Start imagining your legs. Begin to feel your feet. Do your feet feel heavy?

The point at which you begin to feel more weight in your feet, you are grounding. Allow yourself to feel that heavy sensation. It's okay. You are doing it correctly even if you do not feel the weight in your feet.

Sit for five to ten minutes. Continue to breathe in and out of your mouth as you would normally. As you get used to doing this, you will find that you can ground yourself in less than two minutes. Ha! That's right. It literally can be a quick fix or a moment to re-center.

There have been moments where I have had calls with entrepreneurs who I could hear were all over the place. Their thoughts were scattered, disjointed and they seemed unsettled. One time last summer I shared this technique over the phone with a woman who was frustrated because she had lost millions of dollars before. In fact, someone I know happened to invest $100K in her 17 years ago. She was talking fast. I stopped her. I asked her permission first. I walked her through how to ground herself in that moment.

She was in New York at the time in a high-rise, 22 stories high. Once she was grounded, I could hear it. It was wild. Her voice actually changed. It was steady. She was calm. She felt better. I felt better for her. So do yourself a favor and try it. If it works for you, then share it with a friend. We all need to recalibrate from time to time. We may not have time to reach a friend or a trusted advisor. Just remember that you are your best source for most things.

If you are, however, dealing with anxiety or other forms of mental health concerns, I highly recommend finding a licensed professional to guide you. This technique is not meant to replace professional help.

#25: KEEPING YOUR HOUSE CLEAN

Your outside is a reflection of your inside.

In Chapter #2, "Organization, Skatterization," I talked about the importance of keeping your environment clean. Your outside is a reflection of your inside.

This also relates to removing people from your life that do not have your best interests at heart. Cleaning house also refers to people, as I mentioned in an earlier chapter. As you get closer and closer to achieving your milestones and eventually your goal, you will find that clarity is a necessity.

Why? Because you have to be able to sift and see beyond what's in front of you. As Keon Parsons, Fine Art Appraiser Keon Parsons & Associates shares with us here:

> Minimalism, less is more. And simplicity means a lot to me. Try to be very specific. My practice is very specific. I am more edified and fulfilled when digging into something deeper and deeply.

#26: PROTECTING YOUR CAPACITY

It's okay to say NO nicely. Now is probably a good time to share with you that I have intentionally set the order of chapters in correspondence with entrepreneurial growth patterns. Provided that you have launched your business and are knocking down milestones along your journey to reaching your intended goal, this chapter is strategically placed.

Following are some better ways to say "NO" from a position of confidence, grace, and strength:

- "No thank you."
- "My apologies, but not at this time, thank you."
- "I am terribly sorry but I am currently focused on completing a project."

As creatives, our brains are going more and usually faster than most. We all only have so much energy in a day. It's important for you to give yourself space around your meetings as well. Try not to schedule your calendar with back-to-back meetings. Sure, it looks cool on your computer screen with all of the various color coding options. But If you are rolling from meeting to meeting without a 10 the 15-minute break in between, that's too much.

During the 2020 pandemic, a lot of people had to migrate from their in-person work office to their home virtual office, taking most of their meetings in front of a screen. It continues to surprise me that corporations and foundations with Human Resource (HR) departments were not following 9-5 office protocols. What I mean by that is this: I talked to more people who were having meetings after 7 p.m.or example, a girlfriend of mine was on a call with me at 9:30 pm, but was still working in the background for a deadline that she had later that night. It's as if companies forgot the importance of break time.

As an entrepreneur, it's up to you to create breaks for yourself. It's up to you to protect your capacity. It's important that you learn this and implement it because as your company continues to grow and there are more demands on your time, you will have already established your mode of operations. Do not take this for granted. When people do not protect their capacity, they find themselves exhausted, they feel less productive, and this will ultimately lead to burnout.

Back in Chapter 3, I shared the story of the social media maven who experienced extreme fatigue. It is important to learn early in your process to establish boundaries around your time. But the key is that you have to do it for yourself. The examples that I shared in Chapter 3 were individuals who worked for themselves. They did not want to miss an opportunity. So I say to you, it's okay to miss a couple of events. Schedule out your opportunities and when you can, make sure you control the scheduling as opposed to someone else leading the determined time.

When you remember to fight for yourself, others will not fight you. They will actually support and respect your process. You want to succeed, right? I want you to succeed. It's like watching the end of a marathon. Have you ever seen the runners come in to the finish line? I have a couple of times. Once I joined my partner in Paris for the marathon. I made it just in time to watch him reach the finish line.

But before he arrived, I watched other people crossing the finish line. It was disturbing to see one body after another breaking down. These were people who, for a very short but arduous moment in time, moved like robots whose charges were running down. Vomit was surging from some. For others, legs were crumbling once they crossed the finish line. Here's my point: finish strong with grace and exuberance.

Don't bury yourself in chaos. Those times will come where you have to race to the finish and will be beaten down. It's okay. Just don't make it your way of doing business. Marathon runners train and some travel to different cities because each race is different. Follow their lead. Keep yourself in shape. Be sure you are eating well and getting enough sleep.

This reminder is about putting your mask on first, just as they instruct us on the airlines. Because when you are so busy pleasing others and not wanting to disappoint them, you are neglecting your vital life force. That life force is what powers you forward. Be sure you take time to power down! Nappers are nicer people!

#27: BURNOUT IS REAL

There are some clear cut signs of burnout. The notion of a side hustle can become a slippery slope for some. People who have a primary job while also developing their business on the side, run the risk of overworking themselves. This is slightly different from juggling. In an earlier chapter, I referenced juggling as a way to maintain a form of balance while managing several aspects of your business, not maintaining several businesses at once.

Job burnout is a special type of work-related stress. Mayo Clinic defines it as, "*A state of physical or emotional exhaustion that also involves a sense of reduced accomplishment and loss of personal identity.*" "Burnout" isn't a medical diagnosis. But whatever the cause, job burnout can affect your physical and mental health.

There used to be a time where I thrived on multiplicity. I don't know that I've ever just done one thing. When I lived in New York, at any given time I had five jobs. People say, "Really? How is that possible?" Well, I had my own painting company called Pretty Painters where I painted individual's interior walls from a healing perspective. I performed Off-

Broadway with the Red Bull Theater Company. I was the Assistant Manager for Hugo Boss in Time Warner Center and also on Fifth Avenue.

I opened up a plant store in Harlem for investors, built it out, designed it and as I shared earlier, I was a Host on HGTV's show *Splurge and Save* back in 2006. I defined myself as I said earlier as a multi-hyphenate. I am successful at multiple disciplines in life. But like anything, as we have "more experience" and we listen to ourselves, we refine our ways.

Burnout is real. I have to say that I didn't experience the extraordinary fatigue that defines burnout. But I am willing to share that I experienced some greater effects of burnout coming out of 2020 into 2021. Sure, I always felt tired. The most disturbing thing for me was my memory. At times, I couldn't seem to form my words. I think I was mostly embarrassed.

I didn't really know what was happening to me. So I didn't really talk about it. But it was apparent in conversations with those who I worked with when I could not recall a very simple name, and they found themselves finishing my sentences. All I know is that I kept saying, "I need a vacation." I watched the person who worked with me go on two vacations when I had not yet had one.

I justified this because neither one of us had salaries commiserate with our skillset. He was a great employee with a wonderful family. I didn't realize at the time that I was sacrificing myself. But when we are leading organizations or we are our business as entrepreneurs, sometimes we are the last ones to really see the detriment that we are causing to ourselves because we are so focused on meeting the needs of others. Consider the insight of George Vukotich, Ph.D.Founding Director, Center for Research in Innovation and Smart Cities —University of Wisconsin-Parkside:

Burnout is real, but too often it is not recognized until too late. Leading an organization means taking care of your people but too often the leader/caretaker has no one to take care of them. Take time to reflect. Find a confidante outside of your organization you can talk to.

#28: FINDING YOUR FOCUS

Choose a job you love and you'll never have to work a day in your life.

CONFUCIUS

Or in the book *The Power of Focus*, Jack Canfield, Mark Victor Hansen and Les Hewitt write, "When you focus most of your time and energy doing the things you are truly brilliant at, you eventually reap big rewards."

I absolutely believe both of these statements to be very true. I'm almost curious, as if I could hear your answer. But after having gotten this far in the book, would you say that you are not only brilliant at what you are doing but you are also doing what you love? Or have you simply created a business where you found a gap and you're solving that problem?

Both questions are not only important to answer but need to both be answered with a resounding "YES!" So ask yourself if you are consciously choosing a job that you love AND you are good at so that you don't have to feel like you are working another day in my life. If the answer is "Yes, you will feel amazing. However, if your answer is "No" then you need to keep searching for the job that blends your passion AND your prowess (aka your skill or expertise in a particular activity or field).

I mentioned earlier in "Managing Family Expectations" that some people think of entrepreneurship as a very selfish endeavor. It may come across as a luxury for some. Or maybe you've just figured out the secret sauce to the age-old wisdom thought leaders figured out early. You get to decide.

You learned how to ground yourself. Apply the grounding technique before you begin this exercise.

I am a list maker. My sister prefers "Pros & Cons." Either way, if you are not sure if you are making the right decision, do this for yourself. Write down what you love doing in one column. Write down what you do not like in another column:

- What's your passion meter read on a scale of 1-10?
- Do you like to travel?
- Are you an Inside or Outside person?
- Standing desk, cubicle or no desk?
- Are you an early bird or a night owl?
- Do you like to drive or be driven?
- Are you the Doer? Or are you seeking outside approval?

Keep your list going. Then once done, check your answers against the company that you have created or plan to create. Does your list of wants match up to work/LOVE of your business?

Don't stop there. Now meditate for ten to fifteen minutes and ask yourself, "What do I want to do? What is best for my highest good?" Wait for an answer. Then listen to yourself and pay attention to what comes up. You just may get what feels like a random phone call that presents you with another opportunity.

It is important to make sure that you are focused on the right endeavor or else you will feel like you are wasting your time. You are not. It took me 28 years to ask myself and listen to what it is I TRULY want. But no one could have told me any different. I am thrilled about the endearing relationships I have established along the way, and the other businesses that I have built. Consider that each experience is a building block upon which you have laid a solid foundation. Everything you have done thus far has prepared you for this moment. Embrace it.

#29: LIVING IN THE MOMENT

Where are you right now? Yes. Literally take a deep breath in and exhale out in this moment, asking yourself, "What am I thinking about? Am I present?" Or were you thinking about next week's schedule, or your upcoming weekend plans?

How often are you not in the moment? By asking yourself these questions it will begin to force you to consider being more present. There's something to be said about the richness of this moment, right here right now. We are all bombarded by noise, the hum of city traffic, the glaring sounds from the TV, commercials, fearful news, and constant social media posts. And then there is often the overriding fear of missing out.

So given all of above, how often are we connected to our bodies? Do you ever stop and think about the beauty of how your heart pumps this nourishing liquid through your veins to keep all of your organs in action? Yeah, why would you stop and think about that? But the reality is that simply as human beings, we are pretty fascinating. Yet we take ourselves and each other for granted.

We don't mean to do this. Living in the moment requires us to address what is real. So many people want to escape or find ways to numb their reality. I bring this up because as Creatives, we are at our best when we are fully engaged in the moment!

Inspiration comes from moment to moment awareness. If you are detached and zooming around in a frenzy of busyness, you could miss it. Opportunities are funny. Sometimes like a taxi, they will circle back and U-Turn to get to you or they will simply keep on going.

We have these amazing bodies/machines that we walk around in. I call it the shell I walk in. I'm fortunate to be graced with this body for all of these years. It has served me well. And I'm doing my best to honor it by maintaining it in the best way possible. I encourage you to find ways to celebrate yourself regularly.

Very much like I recommended you take time for your family members, be sure to do the same for yourself. It's about you protecting your capacity with yourself as well. Does a weekly workout keep you in the moment? Maybe you have a monthly ritual where you find time to connect with nature. Take a hike.

Taking time to be in the moment does not cost anything. Museums have opened back up (at least at the writing of this book) and provide a significant amount of space to socially distance while enjoying the wonders of other creatives. Get out and listen to some live music. Try focusing on the various instruments and discerning where the sounds are coming from. Catch how many times your brain wanders off, and draw it back to the present moment with the sounds of the music.

A dear new friend makes candles. I love the practice of pouring the wax and the scent that settles in. I also love the illumination of the light both in the day and the night. Next time you have a candle burning, check out the flame. How it waves back and forth, and the color variations.

Find your own ways to draw yourself into the current

moment. I have a dog and sometimes, it's the way he looks at me that reminds me to be present for him. Our furry family friends live in the moment all of the time. Lastly, take yourself to a mirror and look at yourself for a while. Focus on your eyes. Give yourself a couple of deep breaths. Enjoy that time with yourself for yourself. It means a lot. If no one else has quality time to give you, give it to yourself. These opportunities will afford you future support when times get stressful. Moreover, they will sharpen your ability to focus.

#30: GETTING BACK ON TRACK

So you've written your list, you've checked it against the vision that you have for your business and you've decided that you're on the right path. Great! You have grounded yourself, meditated and now, are you living more in the moment? The slight distinction is that in Chapter 6, "Sticky, Is Your Vision Valuable?" you were testing your idea against the market. Now I have suggested that you check it against your passion meter to determine if this is a company that will sustain you.

Getting back on track is about reassessing every now and then where you are in your process. It affords you the opportunity to decide the direction in which you want to go from here forward. Again, you're designing your business, your life. It's always okay to check in with your circle of success.

But ultimately you're making the decisions about the choices you make. Those decisions will impact those around you. I have several books that I go back to throughout the years and at different times in my life. My intention is that hopefully this book will serve you at different points in your journey. That you may realize that, "That's right. I got off track." Being a creative entrepreneur takes a lot of courage. Some of the techniques that I've shared with you may help you recalibrate and realign back to your life's mission. Here is some wisdom shared by Alex Pissios~ Owner of Cinespace Chicago Film Studio

> 'I'm 49 and I got back on track. I was 35 with a family when I received a Red eviction notice on my Hawthorn Woods home. I was a developer of residential properties on the North and West Sides, I'd been taken down by the real estate crash of the 2000s. I owed creditors $13 million. I thought my career was finished, and my old associates were no longer friends. My wife had to go back to work as a dental hygienist, and I became the stay-at-home dad with nothing else to do but change diapers and drive the kids to school. Then something remarkable happened.
>
> Before the market crashed back in 2008 I got an invite to a cousin's wedding in Toronto. To make a longer story shorter, my uncle Nick Mirkopoulos covered the cost of my $25,000 court filings and then proceeded to give me an assignment. Cinespace was looking to open in the US. My uncle wrote me a check to purchase what is now over 1M Square Feet with over 60+ acres. Now my company is worth more than numbers, it's now a letter... "B.
>
> When Saudia asked me if she should build a film studio, I asked her, "Are you sure you want in on this? This is a crazy business!" I told her, "Get someone to write you a check. DO NOT CARRY A MORTGAGE. It will kill your business." That's how so many studios die. My Uncle Nick framed my RED eviction notice and told me to never forget. It sits on my wall as a reminder to this day!"

#31: CREATING YOUR LIFE'S MISSION STATEMENT

In all of the 15+ years I've consulted with organizations, helping them to create a mission statement and follow through with educational programs that meet the mission, it was only three years ago that I wrote my first "Life's Mission Statement." It's never too late.

It is as simple or as complicated as you want to make it. I recommend, however, that you keep it to two or three sentences. This will encourage you to use your words wisely. Less is more and believe it or not, less words with more specificity will mean more. This way the Universe will not get confused.

Every chapter that has led up to this point was preparing you for this moment. So embrace it. Take your time with it. Start to ideate around what is most important to you. Ask a friend who knows you well or a mentor advisor to assist you. I suggest this only because you can lean on their expertise to see beyond your experience and guide you a little better. However, it is *your* life's mission statement, so if their advice does not align with your gut, do not write it down.

Read it every day. Your life's mission will quietly guide your decisions. Just as I have suggested you check your list against your vision, check your mission statement against your company goals. Does your life's mission statement share values with your company's mission statement?

Consider this, your life's mission statement is a wide breadth about what you believe your role here is in life. You may create many companies and innovations over the course of your lifetime. So then you may find that your life and company core values have a shared through-line but the business you create may have various functions.

For example, your Life's mission statement may be to eradicate global poverty by encouraging awareness of universal family and child protection for underserved communities. While your business's mission may be to raise money to direct financial resources to early childhood community education programs on the South and West Side. Here is some wisdom shared by Ron Wexler ~NextGen Growth Partners~ Director of Business & Talent Development:

> Remember grade school when your English teacher taught you how to write a paper? Conclusion in the first sentence and then present three supporting arguments to support your conclusion. A mentor challenged me to live my life in a similar manner. He recommended I craft a life mission statement and only take on commitments if they were consistent with my values. I landed on: "Live an extraordinary life by taking the path least traveled, consistently pursuing your potential, and helping others achieve greatness."
>
> Instead of worrying about fancy job titles, income or prestige I now wake up every morning wondering how many people I will help today. Having a mission statement has

helped me become more intentional with my time and given my life more purpose. Every morning I start my day by reading my mission statement and core values. It sets the tone for the rest of the day, and is helping me develop a growth mindset.

#32: AMPLIFY YOUR VISION

Modern technology allows us to promote what it is that we do or that we love. Social media has made it extremely easy with Instagram posts, Tik-Tok and Twitch. So many of these new technologies arise so often I can't keep up with all of them. But what I would say is that for an emerging entrepreneur or a seasoned business owner, it's in your best interest to utilize these tools that are free.

Canva is my new favorite. I feel for all of my PR and marketing company friends out there who have to compete for what now has been made free to online users. Canva allows you to create marketing campaigns to push out on social media. Send a birthday card to a friend or create a business presentation. It's a full-service one-stop marketing shop.

What I like most about it is that you can create a template that you can make slight changes or updates to on a regular basis. For brand recognition, I strongly believe in continuity. It's important for people to start to recognize your brand in the midst of everyone else's. So make it fun and eye-catching.

There are other services out there. Find what works best for you. Before you amplify anything, you want to make sure that what you are putting out into the world is in alignment with your values, your mission and meets your brand requirements. I mentioned earlier that I might have a tinge of OCD. At the very least, I am learning to release my inner control freak. Ha! I like fonts to be consistent, and be sure to double- and even triple-check your spelling and dates for events.

Once you have created your business marketing tools, sometimes referred to as "collateral," beta test them. Share them with some friends and get their honest feedback. I let people know I want honest feedback. It's the only kind that really counts. I do not need an ego stroke. Once you have consensus among those you trust, including advisers and your circle of success, then shoot it out to the moon! Amplify it to every degree that is appropriate.

Timing is interesting, right? Sometimes people say, "Well, I don't want somebody to take my idea." Others will say that ideas are out there floating around and are for the taking. So don't worry about somebody else taking your idea because really, only you can execute your vision successfully!

#33: SHORING UP YOUR SUCCESS

How do you define success? What is the vision that you set forth? Does success mean you are able to run your business, turn a profit, pay your mortgages, pay for your children's tuitions and take annual vacations? Does success mean you have multiple residences, both a coastal and a rural farm in Montana with horses, travel the world, hobnobbing with socialites and celebrities on your annual vacations?

Not everyone wants to be famous. Some people define success as living a quiet, fulfilling life that is meaningful for them. There is no judgment either way. Some people hear a different calling. They believe that their voice, likeness, and image have value, and therefore created businesses that command more attention to them as a persona. Regardless of what anyone else recommends, you have to be clear with YOU. What do YOU want? How do YOU believe it's in the best interests of you and your family too, as well as for your business?

The business that you create is much like a child. You birth it, nurture it. Clearly, I do not have any children. I ask that my birth mothers out there not take offense to my metaphor. Once you have taught it how to crawl, then walk, and other people like employees are taking care of it, and depending on how large the business becomes, with potential stakeholders, advisors, and board members, your vision becomes that which you initially created.

But over time, it takes on a life of its own. It graduates. And for this very reason, much like how a mother feels later in life, we just want to know that we have raised the business right, that it serves the community, and meets its mission for the highest good yielding great returns on our investment. So keep learning and keep feeding your vision, because like our friend Mr. Pissios experienced, once you get back on track, you have no idea how numbers can turn into letters until they do!

I trust that the guidance in this book has provided you with the tools needed for your personal evolution. Now you have 33 extra skills as a creative entrepreneur to make your business sustainably successful and not screw up. This ensures that you are shored up for success.

WHY 33 WAYS?

This series started as a unique vision that came to Networlding Publishing President Melissa G. Wilson. Her vision was to create an easy-to-read book series focused on the best business practices related to various subjects.

Melissa shares the following message through her many speaking engagements, social media, and marketing channels: "The 33 *Ways* series is a passion project providing the most important advice for the many business problems that keep us up at night."

Focused on building a vibrant book series, Melissa is constantly looking for leading experts in every business niche to share their unique wisdom in their 33 *Ways* books with you. In its first year, the series grew to include eleven books.

One of the best benefits of the series has been the support network Melissa created for the authors to continuously support one another, helping them share their broader wisdom through their respective networks.

As Melissa shares often about the significance of the number three:

> Others might find it strange, but I've always loved the number three. It carries spiritual significance for me. I can't go a week without seeing that number appear in my everyday life—through license plates, grocery bills, phone numbers, and so on, the number keeps showing up as a reminder to keep the series going to provide simple, powerful, and, primarily, easy-to-implement solutions that this series seeks to provide its readers.

All the authors in this series have one unique thing in common: the passion for making a difference in the lives of others, along with the robust desire to share their wisdom with as many eager learners as possible. Melissa calls this "The 33 Ways Great Invitation!"

BUT WAIT! THERE'S MORE!

I'd love to hear from you. This is my first swing at writing. I want to know what you think about this book. You can email me at saudiaauthorspeaker@gmail.com. Let others know what you think by leaving an honest review wherever you bought it. Your kind review will help other people find the book as well!

Check out my weekly talk show, "Reel to Real," on my Redwood Cove Media Youtube page. We keep it real and up to date. This is a great time to listen to other thought leader guests talk about their entrepreneur journey and share business tips for success. If you would like to be a guest on our Reel to Real, send me an email with your show suggestions.

Invite me to come and speak in person or virtually. Following are four of my top subjects:

- The Art of Creative Nudges
- Habits of the Creative Mind
- Relationship Building for Creative
- How Creatives Can Get Funding

For speaking engagements contact me at: saudiaauthorspeaker@gmail.com.

The Great Exchange - A Great Opportunity

Finally, join the **Great Exchange Movement Practice Circles** with me. Meet other readers who are also want-to-be authors. This gives emerging creatives to read and get new-author insights and wisdom on book writing, publishing, and marketing.

ABOUT THE AUTHOR

Saudia Davis is a multi-entrepreneur, Emmy Award-winning producer, developer, creative entrepreneur, and creative strategist with over 25 years of experience in the creative sector focused on the business of entertainment. The combination of her corporate background, passion for ideation, connectivity, problem-solving and resource development enable her to generate impact. Saudia is applauded for a 1000-seat theatre development, Kehrein Center for the Arts, KCA in Chicago's Austin neighborhood, where she also created the vision for how the venue operates in community engagement. She creates places for creatives to play on stage and on camera.

Saudia has worked with Academy Award, Grammy Award, Tony Award, and Clio Award-winning talent like Roman Coppola, Randy Fletcher, Spike Lee, Janusz Kaminski, Bob Merlotti, and others early. Francis Ford Coppola gave her the best advice that guides how she does business to this day. She plays the upright bass.

facebook.com/saudia.davis.3

instagram.com/saudiadavis

linkedin.com/in/saudiadavis

ACKNOWLEDGMENTS

First and foremost, I want to give Glory and Grace to the Almighty, Omnipresent, Omnipotent, All-knowing Source I call God. Thank you for your cover. I have faith in your favor Father. I know you are with me.

Without my parents, who chose to marry each other twice because their love was so strong, they had me on their second time around. Thank you, Mom, for always supporting me as your creative daughter. To my father, I am so proud of you and all of your gifts that grew in me. To my sister, who has always been my inspiration and who set the high bar for which I strove to reach. The eleven years between us have disappeared, and I love our sisterhood, our friendship, and at times my mentorship to you. To my brother-in-law, who has been consistent, a brilliant man, an amazing father, and a great husband to my sister. Alexandra and Brianna, you stole my heart at birth. Harv, you are an amazing man and always there for me.

I appreciate you more than words can express for being the only Dad in my life. Harley, Ashley, Holden, and Asha, I love you. Lucy Lehman, you are family, you are my friend, and I am so grateful to your homemade chocolate chip cookies and stately dinners that you cook for politicians, game-changers, innovators and me. Ken, one day, god willing, I will get married. I love you both to the moon! Zsa Zsa, you are my sister forever. Nadine and Dr. Cedric Sheppard family near and far forever! G Reid, whatcha tellin' me? I miss you, GRANDDADDY! *That's Not Funny!*

Melissa G Wilson, you are more than my publisher. To say thank you is not enough. You have been encouraging me to put my thoughts and experiences down as an author for years. Our worlds collided. These incredible experiences continue to evolve. I have to share that Melissa said to me pre-covid in 2020 Saudia, we have to make you very wealthy so that we can change the world. So let's get to it!

Thanks to Fred Siegman, The Serial ConnectorTM, my *super mentor* who unlocked the *superpower connector* in me. Who knew? You provided me with the manual for this connector mind I had been using. Just a bit of refinement and look at how it works now. It's because of you that I know Bob Gabriel and Melissa, and Billy Dexter. Thank you, Mackenzie Scott, for making the world a better place. I look forward to meeting you really soon.

To my friends who have supported me through good times, fun times, and sad fucked up shit, I LOVE YOU. Tarrey Torae sista friend and J. Ivy, you already know I'm talking to you. Your love inspires me to know that it is possible. Mattie, your years of spiritual guidance and friendship mean the world to me. Ernie Wong, you have always demonstrated your belief in my ability by putting me forward, keeping me in the rooms where I need to be to advance. Kayla Jones, girlfriend, business partner, and fellow producer, I am proud of the mother you have become and the lovely wife you are to Marc. Michelle Dixon, thanks for keeping my hair tight and me looking like the multi-million dollars that I plan to raise this year. Christine Stepp, you keep me moving, sis! Verett Mims, you keep me laughing and fabulous. Thomas McElroy, you are the finest of gentle giants, my friend. Thank you, Theaster, for always providing the space for me to take space. Your vision and what you create continues to inspire me. Thank you, Scott Goodman, for SAYING YES. I look forward to building with you. Ghian Foreman, you are "***too tuff.*** "Keon, thanks for your loving wisdom and friendship. Coach K, you keep me grounded, on track and our spiritual connection is what I prayed for. You already know... *Still.* Thanks, Ellington Robinson, for insisting I go to Amy Sherald's first solo show in Chicago. Thanks, Amy, for sharing your gift of painting with us all, especially that one night with me and Keon at the Soho house. Kahil El'zabar and Lucy Slavinsky, you are the flyest couple that means the world to me. Your spiritual, creative practice has left an indelible imprint around the world and on me. Genevive, tech innovator, opera singer, and pilot, mother of twins, and wife. You are always there. Thank you, next time I will fly with you! Ron Wexler, since the day you told me that I have the ability to raise $500M I've been trying to figure it out.

Ed, Sharon, Gordon, Emron, Mrs. Glover, Steven Saunders, Mary Patt, Rich Daniels, Amy Sudan, and the Entire Wight construction team, thank you for your dedication and support in bringing our Baby, the KCA, to life. Thank you, Andy Wight, of Lookingglass Theatre Company, for believing in my vision and giving me the green light. Thanks to Rahm Emmanuel for allocating $1M to our little theatre on the West side, and thank you, Amy, for passing along all of my messages! Suellen, your mentorship and guidance are forever ingrained in me. Thank you friend.

Thanks, Roman Coppola, for choosing me to be your Talent in your first music video. That experience changed the direction of my life. Thanks for having such a cool dad who showed up on set and shared sage wisdom with me. Francis Ford Coppola, I wish I could tell you to your face, but I do not know how to get in contact. First, you asked, *can I sit next to you?* Then you asked me, *do you want to be in this business?* With my yes, you told me, *stay sweet, you are so sweet, don't let anyone change that, if you stay sweet the way you are, you will have a long career in this business, because people in our business only work with people they like.* I was 17, and from that point forward, I have made conscious decisions to stay sweet. I do my best to build lasting, meaningful connections.

Thank you, Deepak Chopra, for redirecting me at a time when I needed it most. I look forward to connecting with you and Rita sometime soon. Roberta Flack, I miss you in my life. Thanks for telling me about how Tina Turner practices T. M. Thank you, Dr. Carla Brown, for being my Transcendental Meditation teacher. Thank you, Bob Roth, for reflecting your joyful light right back at me. I will always appreciate your introduction to Arriana Huffington.

To all of the quote contributors, I respect you beyond expression. I am so proud to call you a friend. Thank you for sharing your experience with the reader of this book. I find myself motivated every time I read your quote contribution.

MORE 33 WAYS

If you enjoyed this book, check out one or more of the books in the series:

If you enjoyed this book, check out one or more of the books in the series following is a list of the other current 33 Ways books:

- "33 Ways Not to Screw Up Consulting"
- "33 Ways Not to Screw Up Your Business Emails"
- "33 Ways Not to Screw Up Your Financial Life"
- "33 Ways Not to Screw Up Creative Entrepreneurship"
- "33 Ways Not to Screw Up Journalism"
- "33 Ways Not to Screw Up Negotiations"
- "33 Ways Not to Screw Up HR"
- "33 Ways Not to Screw Up a Thought Leadership Book - (Free at www.networlding.com
- "33 Ways Not to Screw Up Cybersecurity"
- "33 Ways Not to Screw Up Hiring Great Talent"
- "33 Ways Not to Screw Up Your Business Podcast"

- "33 Ways Not to Screw Up Being a Women in Tech"

Finally, check out our website at: www.33waysseries.com

Made in the USA
Monee, IL
02 March 2024

54074072R00075